To Dam —

Hope you like the book!

Best,

"An outstanding book! In a series of riveting chapters, Sam Weinman portrays spectacular failures—huge, public failures—that helped people grow instead of crushing them. You will be inspired."

—Carol S. Dweck, PhD,
New York Times bestselling author of *Mindset*

"Because we live in a country where our most admired citizens are labeled 'winners,' we often fail to appreciate the tremendous value of defeat. Well, thank goodness for Sam Weinman, whose ode to dropping the ball, missing the shot, failing to rise to the occasion is a beautiful—and important—reminder that second place often trumps first. A blissful read."

—Jeff Pearlman,
bestselling author of *The Bad Guys Won*

"Sam Weinman took on a fascinating challenge when he decided to look into how people deal with loss—*not* just in sports, but in many walks of life. His reporting is thorough and insightful, allowing the reader a view of how those who are the best at what they do deal—and grow from—defeat."

—John Feinstein,
bestselling author of *A Season on the Brink*

"What's the thread that unites the highest performers in sports, business, and life? They've all faced failure and defeat . . . and emerged stronger for the experience. Sam Weinman takes readers on an entertaining journey that shows how getting knocked down is part of all of our lives, and how each of us can grow and learn from the experience."

—Mark McClusky,
bestselling author of *Faster, Higher, Stronger*

"Sam Weinman will have to do his own 'winning from losing' in some other forum, because his book is terrific. And, although its genesis was in sports, it's really about how to be a better, happier, and more self-aware person."

—David Owen,
staff writer, *The New Yorker*

"We always hear and read a great deal about winning and the joy of success. *Win at Losing* is all about the other side of winning and the truth that no one wins without losing many times. Learning from losing is a big part of success. *Win at Losing* is a wonderful read."

—Bob Rotella, PhD,
bestselling author of *Golf Is Not a Game of Perfect*

WIN AT LOSING

WIN
AT
LOSING

How Our Biggest
Setbacks Can Lead to
Our Greatest Gains

SAM WEINMAN

A TarcherPerigee Book

tarcherperigee

An imprint of Penguin Random House LLC
375 Hudson Street
New York, New York 10014

Most TarcherPerigee books are available at special quantity discounts for bulk
purchase for sales promotions, premiums, fund-raising, and educational needs.
Special books or book excerpts also can be created to fit specific needs. For
details, write: SpecialMarkets@penguinrandomhouse.com.

ISBN 9780143109587

Printed in the United States of America
1   3   5   7   9   10   8   6   4   2

Book design by Katy Riegel

For Lisa, Charlie, and Will

Contents

WIN AT LOSING

1

How We Win from Losing (and Occasionally Lose from Winning)

The greatest glory in living lies not in never falling,
but in rising every time we fall.
—OLIVER GOLDSMITH

THE MOST IMPORTANT sporting event I ever attended was a kids' tennis match on an August afternoon. This might seem odd coming from a sportswriter who has covered World Series and Stanley Cup Finals and dozens of major golf championships. But none of those events involved my kid. And none led me down this curious road of talking to everyone from professional athletes to CEOs to presidential candidates about their most crushing defeats. That's the road that led me here.

But first there was a tennis match on a quiet late-summer day. There was no press. There were only a handful of spectators. And the only real drama came at the end when my oldest son essentially lost it.

I should explain: Charlie is a pretty good tennis player. Approaching eleven, he has everything down—the two-handed backhand, the open-stance forehand, the emphatic little grunt with every stroke. Charlie couldn't tell you the reason one grunts when playing tennis. But he knows that Rafael Nadal grunts, so the conversation ends there.

This is how it usually works with him. About a year ago, Charlie talked us into getting him a blue Nike headband like the one Nadal wears, and now whenever he misplaces it, he reacts as if he's missing a kidney. "Where's my headband?" he'll ask before a match, tearing frantically through the house. "I can't play without my headband!"

Over the course of that summer, as Charlie would punctuate forehand winners with Nadal uppercuts, the other kids around the tennis court took to calling him Rafa. Charlie ate it up—so much, in fact, that if in mixed company I dared to call him anything else, I might as well have announced he still wet the bed.

"*Rafa*," he'd correct me.

"Right," I'd say. "Sorry."

When it came time for our club's junior tournament, Charlie progressed through the early portion of the ten-and-under bracket with enough ease that he began thinking ahead to the final. We both did, actually, although outwardly I was saying all the right "dad" things: Respect your opponent; one match at a time; it's important to just have fun. In the semifinal, when he matched up against a timid, freckly kid named Jake, Charlie bounced onto the court confidently, perhaps thinking that if he wrapped up the win with enough time to spare, he could sneak in a swim and a candy bar before dinner. Seated on the deck overlooking the tennis courts, my wife, Lisa, and I made small talk with Jake's mom and feigned indifference through the first part of the match. *Oh, are they keeping score? How cute!* We anticipated a short match.

But as play unfolded, nothing went right. Charlie placed backhands into the corner, and Jake hunted them down, sometimes even passing Charlie with a winner of his own. Serving, never a strength for my son, was now an ordeal, with Charlie at one point forfeiting an entire game by sending eight consecutive balls into the net. On the deck, Lisa continued to indulge Jake's mom in conversation, but I couldn't hear them anymore. I was entranced. As I watched my son, I could see his anxiety level rise—the hurried tosses, the twitchy fiddling with his racket, the occasional look heavenward when he sailed another shot long, as if God had suddenly taken interest in a ten-year-old's tennis match and was siding squarely with Jake.

By the final game, Charlie was flat-footed and waving passively at the ball. On the final point his forehand bounced *before* the net and onto Jake's side, and Jake briefly weighed whether he should play it. It didn't matter; the match was over in twenty minutes. Charlie lost 6–1.

When Jake approached the net with his hand extended, Charlie shuffled forward to weakly reciprocate, looking past his opponent the whole time. Then he tore off his headband, flung his racket at my feet as I approached, and ran toward the parking lot.

"Charlie!" I hissed in a sort of scream-whisper, the same type of urgent yet polite tone you might use to ask someone to fetch you a roll of toilet paper. "Come back!"

Charlie turned toward me, his face streaked with tears.

"I'm never playing tennis again!" he said. "That's it!"

"That's it?" I said. "You're retiring? Will there be a press conference?"

"Stop, Dad," he said. "It's not funny."

It went on like that for a little while, Charlie swearing off tennis, me summoning some of my best "It's only a game—you'll learn from this" material. Though I still hadn't talked him out of retirement, I eventually convinced him to gather his racket and head to the car while I went to find Lisa, who had said good-bye to Jake and his mom and was now waiting for me under the awning by the tennis court. Lisa and I have been married for fifteen years and have been friends since the fifth grade. She knows all my looks, and I know most of hers, and as I walked toward her, she offered a faint smile in the "What have we gotten ourselves into?" vein. Then she finally spoke.

"My God," she said. "He's *you*."

So this book began with a tennis match. In watching Charlie unravel over something so insignificant, I started to think about how learning to lose is an acquired skill, like juggling or parallel parking. It contradicts our most basic nature because everything in our DNA has taught us to want to win and hate to lose. After all, at one point in our history, winning was about more than tennis matches. It was about securing food and shelter and not letting the neighborhood pack of wolves make off with one of your kids. You've heard that Vince Lombardi line "Winning isn't everything. It's the only thing." The context was football, but for a great portion of human existence, it could have been describing the simple struggle to survive.

Now, though, we lose and usually live to tell about it. We lose in sports, and we lose in our careers, and we lose out on that house with the perfect backyard we were certain we were going to get. Some of us are losing our hair, although we'd prefer not to talk about that. Over the course of any given year, we probably lose in a thousand different ways, and as painful and inconvenient as those losses might be, we still have a say in how we handle them. We too often overlook that last part.

This is a truth I've come to appreciate not only as a father of two sports-mad boys but also as someone who's had his own frequent dalliances with failure. My wife's contention that Charlie in the teary aftermath of his tennis match is a miniature version of me is true, but only to an extent. I still struggle with losing in its various forms: in men's league hockey games, in golf matches for five dollars, and as an editor when I see the competition come up with a story we don't have. My authority in writing this book does not stem from the graceful and admirable ways I've lost in my life but rather the opposite. I've thrown my racket and slammed my fist on my desk, and on one occasion I slung my varsity jacket into a puddle of mud after a bad pass cost my high school hockey team our season. Once, stuck in a newspaper job, I was awaiting word about a plum job I was on the short list for getting. It was my birthday, and Lisa and I were headed out the door for dinner. When the email came that the job went to someone else, I sat down at our kitchen table and cried.

The difference now is I also see that losing can serve in ways winning never can. Losing has taught me and toughened me and forced me to address the very shortcomings that got me in trouble in the first place. That bad pass I made at the end of my junior year in high school inspired me to get stronger and fitter, and it led to a senior year in which I emerged a different player. That plum job I didn't get was inspiration to develop the skills that led to an even better opportunity later.

Looking outside myself, I've also come to realize that the people I'm most impressed by are not the ones who appear to float through life but those whose weaknesses and failures are exposed in all sorts of undignified ways and yet they emerge stronger as a result: golfers who've blown tournaments, politicians who've botched elections, the bookstore owner who has struggled to pay his bills for decades and has only recently begun to turn a profit. What I've found is that the people who've approached their failures honestly and constructively are often able to point to tangible benefits of those losses. The impact of this can be profound: The more we can embrace the upside of losing, the healthier our perspective toward whatever is in front of us, the less encumbered we are by fear.

Although my interest in how we handle losing began with a personal challenge, I saw it as a challenge that permeated every segment of our society. And it was in recognizing the thread between my family's modest struggles and the bigger, bolder stories that exist elsewhere that I decided to dive in headfirst. I sought out Olympians and politicians, entertainers and Internet startup CEOs. Their versions of losing vary—lost games, failed political campaigns, businesses and careers dissolved in flames—and may seem unrelated at first glance. But there are similarities as well, and it was upon consulting a wide swath of experts that I learned there is not only an art to losing but a great deal of science, too. I saw there is a way to not only tolerate setbacks but also use them as a foundation for future success—to win, if you will, at losing.

I'd love to tell you I contemplated all this while driving away from the tennis courts that day, but more likely I was thinking about dinner and whether I needed to stop for beer. But the image of Charlie's frustration lingered. I had taught my son a forehand and a backhand, and he knew exactly where to stand when receiving at 30–15. Yet there was still much for both of us to learn about coping with the swirling emotions that come with defeat.

No one sets out to be a good loser, in the same way that no one sets out to be an ex-husband. I used to think of losing as one would curing a hangover or avoiding prosecution: If you've achieved a level of proficiency at it, you probably ought to consider what that says.

You may recall Super Bowl 50, when the Denver Broncos upset the Carolina Panthers, and Carolina's star quarterback, Cam Newton, was so despondent he walked out of his postgame press conference. The next day he explained his reasoning, "Show me a good loser and I'll show you a loser."

I've come to abhor that sentiment to the point that I now think being a good loser is exactly what we should aspire to be. Being a good loser does not denote some hapless resignation. It implies perspective and resilience and the quiet confidence that the world will not crumble around you just because of a fleeting setback.

There are all kinds of stories about athletes whose abundant desire to win carried over to the most mundane tasks. At airports, Michael Jordan would bet his teammates whose bag would shoot out of the carousel first. Jordan was said to revel in winning, less because he needed to prove his baggage claim prowess and more because, like Cam Newton, he didn't want any more experience with losing than he absolutely needed.

Trivial as it sounds, Jordan was doing himself a disservice. There is in fact merit to this sort of experience, and he should know. As a high school sophomore, Jordan was famously cut from the varsity basketball team, and he channeled that disappointment into a competitive fire that burned for decades. Later, when his Chicago Bulls stumbled in the playoffs each spring against the more experienced Detroit Pistons, Jordan used the lessons from those losses to help transform the Bulls into a dynasty.

The Bulls would win six NBA championships over the next eight years, and Jordan, who also won an NCAA title and two Olympic gold medals, would become known as the consummate winner in basketball, if not all of sports. But success brought complications as well, many of which persisted into retirement. Jordan became so obsessed with winning and so uneasy with losing that he struggled to find a comparable outlet now that he had hit middle age and was incapable of replicating the same level of success he had as a player. The writer Wright Thompson had rare access to Jordan and his inner circle for a 2014 profile in *ESPN the Magazine,* and he depicted the basketball legend in the years following his retirement as unfulfilled and restless.

"There's no way to measure these things, but there's a strong case to be made that Jordan is the most intense competitor on the planet. He's in the conversation, at the very least, and now he has been reduced to grasping for outlets for this competitive rage," Thompson writes in "Michael Jordan Has Not Left the Building." "His self-esteem has always been, as he says, 'tied directly to the game.' Without it, he feels adrift. 'Who am I? What am I doing?'"

By Thompson's account, Jordan's model was unsustainable. Beyond deriving outsized satisfaction from the games he won, he had so distanced himself from the sensation of failure that he had no road map for how to react when his post-Bulls career proved rocky. To Dr. Jerry Brodlie, a noted family psychologist in Greenwich, Connecticut, this Jordan was an extreme version of the teenager who thinks he can do no wrong and then struggles mightily once he does. "It's like he's this golden kid who develops an inflated sense of self," Brodlie says. "Ultimately, these are the kids who have a really hard time when whatever makes them special is taken away."

In his celebrated commencement address at Kenyon College in 2005, the late author David Foster Wallace detailed the perils of placing unhealthy value in something as tenuous as money, beauty, or glory. "Worship power, you will end up feeling weak and afraid, and you will need ever more power over others to numb you to your own fear," Wallace said.

The point isn't that you should strive for mediocrity, and heaven help me if my argument is based on the pitfalls of becoming a multimillionaire icon. But both Brodlie and Wallace arrive at the same place: uninterrupted success is a fantasy. The absence of certain humbling elements in our lives makes us more vulnerable in the long run. From there it stands to reason that losing is something not only that we should tolerate but also that we *need*.

"We all avoid the things we don't want to deal with, and that includes anything related to losing," says Dr. Jonathan Fader, a psychologist and author of the book *Life as Sport*, which seeks to implement many principles of sports psychology in everyday life situations. "The idea is to practice how to deal with unwanted consequences. The whole promise of sports psychology is for you to inoculate yourself for when things go bad."

Fader asserts that whether it's sports or business or something else entirely, it's a mistake to try to shield yourself from failure, for reasons that should be apparent: Unless you become the first person in the history of humankind to go through life without setbacks, you're better served having a sense of how to respond when things fall apart on you, because at some point they will. Fader uses the phrase "contingency management" to describe our ability to deal with these unforeseen challenges. He likens it to taking the same route to drive to work each day but then realizing your usual route is blocked. If you've had to deal with this sort of thing before, chances are you know of an alternate way and will adjust accordingly. Otherwise you're paralyzed.

"Imagine a world where for every negative result, we just sat in our car [not moving]," Fader says.

As a doctor, he has worked for years with a number of professional athletes, including members of the New York Mets, and he says the mentally strongest among them are the ones who endure a disappointment and effectively move on. In *Life as Sport* Fader describes a veteran pitcher who followed a specific routine after giving up a home run.

"Whenever I get rocked and somebody hit one out, I get the new ball back from the umpire and I concentrate on rotating it in my glove while counting backwards from twenty to one," the pitcher told Fader. "That helps me breathe right and stay in the moment so I can give my complete attention to the next pitch."

The pitcher could avoid facing the possibility of a negative outcome. He instead accepts reality: *Every* pitcher gives up home runs, so he might as well know beforehand how he's going to deal when giving up his.

As an editor at *Golf Digest*, I see this dynamic in golf

often. Butch Harmon, viewed by many as the best golf instructor in the world, points to pros Phil Mickelson and Dustin Johnson as the two current players who are best equipped to rebound from disappointment. Why? Because they've both had a lot of practice. Mickelson went 0 for 46 in major championships before finally winning his first, and Johnson had several excruciating close calls in golf's biggest tournaments before his own breakthrough in the 2016 US Open. Harmon compares both to NFL defensive backs who get beat for touchdowns on deep routes, yet line up for the next play as if nothing ever happened. Because both Mickelson and Johnson have embraced the opportunity to learn from their mistakes, both have repeatedly rallied from disappointing tournaments, often giving themselves a chance to win their next time out. By contrast, Harmon cites those golfers who burst onto the professional tour, win big tournaments early in their careers, but struggle in pulling themselves out of their first rough patch. For those players, Harmon theorizes, success conspires against them.

"Sometimes losing the tournament is better than winning them early because you learn from it," Harmon tells me as we stand on the driving range of a PGA Tour event in New Jersey. "Sometimes guys get out here and they do so well, and then you wonder what happened to them. Well, it came too easy. And all of a sudden when it's not so easy, they don't know how to deal with it."

Consider a recent example: when Jordan Spieth lost the 2016 Masters Tournament by blowing a five-shot lead with nine holes to play. Spieth was twenty-two and coming off a dream season in which he had won both the 2015 Masters and US Open. By the time he teed off that Sunday at Augusta National, he had led golf's most prestigious tournament for seven consecutive rounds. Yet as devastating as his Masters collapse was, there was an argument that it came at just the right time in his development, a sentiment championed by Jack Nicklaus, who said he came to appreciate a comparable loss that he suffered in the 1960 US Open when he was still an amateur. Winning that tournament, Nicklaus said, would have cut into the motivation that later turned him into the greatest golfer of all time.

"In many ways I'm not sure that it isn't a good thing for [Spieth]," Nicklaus told reporters at a press conference shortly after the Masters. "What I mean by that is that he's twenty-two years old. To win a Masters twice at twenty-two years old, that puts him right at the top of everything. Winning it twice might take away some of that focus. [It's the same thing if] I had won the US Open when I was an amateur in 1960. I might not have continued to work."

You'll notice I like to reference sports. I blame this partly on my sports-centric existence—or extended adolescence as some members of my family might describe it. Most men my age see their ties to sports start to fray over time, but mine have only grown stronger. In school I was a frustrated athlete and a fan. But then my career became inextricably tied to sports. Starting out covering sports for newspapers before moving to *Golf Digest*, I've chronicled losing at every level: high school basketball games where kids can't string together two words before breaking into sobs; NHL seasons that end with team members packing away the items in their lockers, some silently wondering if their careers are now over. In professional golf, most tournaments end with 155 losers and only one winner, a long-odds existence that forces participants to define success creatively. Naturally, when Lisa and I had kids, both our boys gravitated early toward sports, to the extent that now should you dare open our front hall closet, you would, in cartoon fashion, be overtaken by an avalanche of cascading balls, rackets, and sticks.

Although broader now, my curiosity about losing began as a sports challenge. The inspiration was my son's lost tennis match, but it just as easily could have been something else. As I write this, I'm an hour removed from coaching a hockey game in which Charlie's team imploded in the third period then started quarreling with one another on the bench, my hot-headed son squarely in the middle. It feels as though I am reminded daily of losing's merit as a worthwhile topic, and I have these two unreasonably competitive boys under my roof to thank. I sometimes wonder if my sons and their friends believe there's a massive scoreboard somewhere keeping tabs of every result over the course of their entire lives, the numbers spinning wildly like the running tally of the national debt. And not just official games, but everything: scrimmages, relay races, schoolyard basketball contests in which boys spend twenty-two minutes picking teams and eight minutes *actually playing*.

Perhaps I was the same way, but I sense it's gotten worse. In the quarter century since I played youth sports, the pressure on kids has grown while the stakes have remained pretty much the same: There are more camps, more summer leagues, more parents who have held their sons and daughters back from kindergarten because some study or another suggests it's key to their success. In the hockey rinks I frequent, there are signs reminding parents not to bang on the glass during their kids' games—worthwhile advice, sure, but sad when you consider it needed to be committed to print. At the end of this road is the same paucity of scholarship offers and professional contracts, yet we've cultivated an environment where the checkpoints along the way have taken on outsized importance. It is because kids and their parents have so wrapped these contests up into their overall feelings of self-worth that I sought to better understand the dynamics of losing.

But I've also recognized that sports are a window into everything else. How we deal with success and failure in sports or other activities early on can be a precursor to how we might navigate more complicated obstacles later. The baseball games we lose at age ten turn into the colleges we don't get into at eighteen, which in turn become lost jobs and marriages and things that are even scarier than that. Of course, it would be contrived to suggest our ability to lose a game and move on will translate to our overcoming life's most daunting challenges with ease. But it can be a start. Think of it this way: If you can't handle things going awry when the stakes are small, you're in for that much rougher a ride when the real challenges start to mount.

"This is an area I speak a great deal about, this whole concept of how you develop resiliency in people," Brodlie, the child psychologist, says. "Over the years you're going to deal with failure, disaster, and painful events, and you have to learn how to get on with life afterward. When you talk about how you develop that, sports is a natural because of the idea you can't always win. That's a given."

The more you care about something, the greater the sting of disappointment, the more profound the lesson. Some people outgrow their investment in sports and move on to other things. Some, like me, never do. In an early correspondence with one of the athletes I talk to in this book, I laid out what I wanted to discuss and made clear that I thought his was more than a "sports story." He agreed.

"It's a 'life story,'" he wrote to me. "It's George Bailey from *It's a Wonderful Life* standing on the bridge, grief and desperation oozing from his face, wondering if there is really a good next step."

Those aren't the words of someone talking about just a game, even if in an indirect way he was. I'll get to his story later, but the important part for now is that because his episode involved real suffering and real emotion, he was a candidate for real growth. Anything less than that and the impact isn't as strong.

It's become apparent that, on a surface level at least, people are more willing to speak to their failures than ever before, in fields beyond just sports. Consider business. Especially in this country, where business owners are protected by bankruptcy laws and there is not the same level of shame attached to failure as in other cultures, there is something even noble about having a dissolved enterprise to call your own. According to Harvard Business School professor Shikhar Ghosh, who has studied the success rate of Internet startups, our enlightened attitude toward failure can be traced back centuries, to when we started as a "country of immigrants, pioneers, and risk takers," Ghosh says. "That spirit still exists today." The idea is that real innovation and progress depend on risk, and thus failure is an inevitable by-product.

But failure alone doesn't guarantee you will benefit in its aftermath. There needs to be an inventory taken of what went wrong and what can be done better as well. The problem is when people want to skip over the hard parts, like those scenes in the movies where the protagonist's struggle to master advanced calculus or train for a marathon is covered in a ninety-second montage put to music. In her book, *Rising Strong*, the author Brené Brown says we live in "a Gilded Age of Failure," where everyone is willing to talk about their setbacks but without an honest assessment of what they really mean.

"We like recovery stories to move quickly through the dark so we can get to the sweeping, redemptive ending," Brown writes. "Embracing failure without acknowledging the real hurt and fear that it can cause, or the complex journey that underlies rising strong, is gold-plating grit. To strip failure of its real emotional consequences is to scrub the concepts of grit and resilience of the very qualities that make them both so important—toughness, doggedness, and perseverance."

Brown's words remind me of those people at the gym who walk on the treadmill for ten minutes, make four trips to the water fountain, then congratulate themselves on the killer workout. In the absence of sweat and discomfort, their spare tire remains stubbornly intact.

The people I talk to in this book were willing to share their stories with me because they *can* point to their own redemptive ending, and it's one they worked hard to achieve. Some enjoyed a follow-up success, but plenty of others didn't. For some the redemptive ending was just a greater understanding of how their setbacks shaped them in positive and serendipitous ways. Given sufficient distance, they were able to look at these episodes through a softer lens. But it was still important to understand the depths of their pain and what precisely they had endured. In the movies, we can get away with skipping the hard parts. In life, that's where we tend to learn the most.

We should probably pause here to talk about the significance of the words we use around these events. There are a bunch of them. Loss. Failure. Disappointment. Setback. As Dr. Jonathan Fader says, they can all fit under the vast umbrella of "unwanted consequences," even if they actually denote different things.

Take that tennis match of Charlie's. For starters, Charlie lost. It was a match between two kids, and he didn't win, and he didn't tie. He lost. That's pretty simple to define on the surface. But it also could be classified a failure in that Charlie had an objective and he was unable to achieve it. He *failed* to beat Jake. He *failed* to get his serve in. He *failed* to manage his frustration as the match got away from him. It was a setback as well in that Charlie had progressed as a player and as a competitor that summer, yet by the time the match was over, he seemed back to where he was before the season began. Naturally, it was a disappointment, too, in that he had his eyes on making it to the tournament finals and even winning, and now he had to reconcile that his tournament was over.

The complicated part is in how these similar-sounding words are actually quite different. For instance, a loss isn't always the result of a failure. Losing can be a simple matter of having something one moment and then not having it the next. We all lose stuff, big and small. We lose direction and hope, and as a result, we might lose a piece of ourselves.

Certainly in the messy aftermath, a loss and a failure are often lumped together because they tend to inspire the same levels of dejection. It's kind of like distinguishing between food poisoning and a stomach flu—at the outset of both, the only thing that matters is you're hunched over feeling awful. But at some point you're going to need to know what you're dealing with.

The distinction between a loss and a failure is perhaps

easiest summarized as follows: There are occasions when we lose—be it a game or a job or whatever—and we need reassurance that the fault isn't ours. A middle management executive might lose his job because his company needs to produce better margins for stockholders. An actress might lose out on a part because she was deemed too short. In the interest of moving on and sparing yourself heartache, recognizing a loss as just a loss is a vital form of self-preservation.

"Losing is simply a fact. Failure is your interpretation of what happened," says Dr. Jim Loehr, a psychologist and the cofounder of the Human Performance Institute in Orlando. "Failure is almost always perceived as something you did wrong. It has a much more indicting component to it."

Loehr's work with patients ranging from professional athletes to corporate executives focuses on framing the events of your life in the most constructive way possible. His point is that *how* you look at what happens is often more important than what actually happens, and thus you need to consider an interpretation that is going to best serve you moving forward. This is tricky, as you might imagine, because you don't want to deceive your mind into believing a distorted reality. Everything needs to be rooted in truth. But even then, there's some flexibility.

"There's a way to digest [loss] in a way that it doesn't leave a hole in your soul," Loehr says. "That serves no purpose. Beating yourself up only serves a purpose if it can be constructive and bring you to higher ground."

The objective is never punishment for the sake of punishment. But Loehr also recognizes there can be danger in giving ourselves *too* quick a pass. In this "Gilded Age of Failure" that the author Brené Brown describes, the opposite of dwelling too long on our mistakes is to dismiss our failures even when we played an active role in them. Say the actress wasn't only too short, but also unprepared. Suppose the laid-off executive was slow to acquire new skills in a changing marketplace. In glossing over our culpability, we are perhaps making ourselves feel better. But we're also denying ourselves the opportunity to capitalize on the experience.

"If you bend the truth, you're not learning from it. We have a tendency to tell ourselves stories to get us through the night, but the important part is to start with the truth, as harsh as it is," Loehr says. "Here are the things that happened. Here's why the business went bankrupt. Let's get all the facts on the table and see what the mistakes are and then decide on the lessons we can move forward with."

It's complicated, I realize, and I wish there were a pair of magic glasses you could pull out of a cereal box to help identify these lessons more clearly. But Loehr's insistence on honesty is the necessary starting point. The clearer your assessment of your experiences, the better positioned you are to interpret them constructively. In the stories that follow, you'll be given examples of failures and losses, often with the same people. That they've all been able to point to some satisfying conclusion is because they've chosen to embrace every part of their history—even the parts most of us would rather forget.

ONE WARM OCTOBER day I visited Reshma Saujani, the CEO of the nonprofit Girls Who Code, at her office in Manhattan. Saujani had recently been named to *Fortune* magazine's list of the forty most influential people in business under the age of forty. The previous week she had introduced Hillary Clinton at a campaign rally. To see Saujani bouncing confidently around that midtown loft, one could easily assume she was used to things going her way.

On the contrary, Saujani describes herself as one of those people for whom "things never came easy." The daughter of Indian immigrants by way of Uganda, Saujani was bullied growing up because of her curious-sounding name, was rejected multiple times by Yale Law School, and had several miscarriages before giving birth to her son in February 2015. These episodes were all crushing at the time, but they also fostered a sense within Saujani that repeated obstacles were just part of the deal. It was an invaluable gift.

"I feel like I've always somewhat embraced struggle and never been afraid of it," Saujani says. "It's just made me stronger. I feel like in some ways it made me feel a little bit shameless in the sense I'm not afraid to ask for things and I'm not afraid to lose. That doesn't mean it doesn't hurt, but it doesn't break me."

In 2010, after graduating from law school and working for a time on Wall Street, Saujani decided she wanted to run for US Congress, challenging the eighteen-year incumbent Carolyn Maloney in the Democratic primary. It was a bold move for a political neophyte—"shameless," as she might put it. Saujani's campaign received a healthy amount of media attention given her outsider status as the first woman of Indian descent to run for US Congress. On the night before Election Day, she called her supporters to tell them things were looking good.

Actually, she never came close—Saujani received just 19 percent of the vote. The outcome was so humiliating she hoped no one would see her as she hailed a cab headed for her Lower East Side apartment, her BlackBerry buzzing with emails she didn't want to acknowledge. Once inside her windowless bedroom, Saujani wanted only to remain under the covers for days.

"I knew people were going to be celebrating my pain," Saujani says. "I was very caught up in what happened—what mistakes did I make? What would I do differently? That was my month of mourning."

In the aftermath of the loss, Saujani's boyfriend (now husband) bought her a dog, mainly, she says, "just to give me some purpose in life and to get out of the bed and shower each day." Slowly she began to piece together a routine. Saujani wrote a book, *Women Who Don't Wait in Line*, in part about the lessons from her failed campaign. Eventually she set out to run again, this time for New York City Public Advocate in 2013. It would have made for a tidy redemptive story, and here Saujani was pretty sure she would win. Except she didn't. This time Saujani lost in even more disheartening fashion, finishing third with just 15 percent of the vote. Once again, she was crushed.

So how did Saujani end up where she is now—overseeing a widely regarded nonprofit that is inspiration for thousands of girls?

The irony of Saujani's losses is that they opened the door for the type of public contribution that likely wouldn't have been possible had she won elected office. Under Saujani's direction as CEO, Girls Who Code taught ten thousand girls computer science in 2015. It has already raised $16 million, aims to reach one million girls by 2020, and is now partnering with Viking to create a series of books about coding written for middle school girls.

That she reached this point, putting her political career aside to focus on something that is arguably more ambitious, is not because she sought to suppress the memories of her disappointments. In fact, it was because Saujani had a predisposition for struggle that she was able to boldly throw herself into a new venture without fear of failure *yet again*. Is that shameless? Yes, but only in the best "So what if I screw up?" sense. She had a keen understanding of how she would react to another possible public face-plant, and as much as her earlier setbacks had truly stung, she knew she was always able to recover.

"When I do something wrong and I make a mistake, that bothers me, and then I get over it quickly," she says. "I'm comfortable with it because once everything I fear happening happens, I realize I'm still standing."

Here is where Saujani hits at the heart of what I'm driving at in this book, and it applies whether you're running for Congress, starting a business, or playing a kid named Jake in a ten-and-under tennis tournament. Saujani did not find success in spite of her past but *because* of it. She lost, felt crummy about it, and took an honest inventory of what she could have done better. Nothing about it was fun, and she wouldn't do it again given the choice. As Brené Brown said in a 2015 interview with *Time*, "When failure doesn't hurt, it's not failure." But for Saujani and countless others, the very painful episodes endured serve as springboards to something more beneficial.

When it comes to teaching my boys, I can cite countless comparable examples of my own—teams I didn't make, games I lost—a whole menu of letdowns that helped me identify and address my most glaring weaknesses. When I think about it, I was better because of them. The process of writing is perhaps the best evidence of this because every story that's ever been kicked back to me ends up being better the second (or third or fourth . . .) time around, to the extent that I'm horrified I ever thought the first version was any good.

Therein lies the genesis for this book. My argument is that we end up learning more from our failures than we do from our successes. And I maintain we're better served listening to those who have lost constructively than those who've simply won. These are the strongest people we know, and in a society still uneasy with failure, their insights are more valuable than ever.

Of course I say all that knowing we can't always be

grateful when first met with these pockets of resistance. Setbacks are annoying: they can eat up hours of your day, and even the most innocuous among them have a nasty habit of knocking your plans off course. I do not expect you, in reading this book, to welcome losing any more than I expect you to enjoy your next colonoscopy. But appreciation of the larger purpose losing can serve should help take away some of the sting.

This is how it began—because I wanted to teach my boys that there is a road we begin on when things don't go our way, and that it may be long and hard, but if we frame it the right way, it can be lined with hope. My expectations were modest. At no point did I think I would cure them of the impulse to throw a tennis racket in a fit of frustration. I've been known to throw one myself. Perspective doesn't prevent the racket from leaving your hand. Perspective is for when it's time to pick it up, and you're left to contemplate what to do next.

2

A Masters in Humility: How Greg Norman Won Fans by Falling on His Face

*I never thought of losing, but now that it's happened,
the only thing is to do it right. That's my obligation to all the
people who believe in me. We all have to take defeats in life.*
—Muhammad Ali

I WORK AT *Golf Digest,* a detail that tends to elicit questions about how I got started in golf. Unlike most of my colleagues, I didn't come from a golf family. My dad played when he was younger, but he quit when he developed a debilitating case of the shanks.* My older brother played a little. The most avid golfer was my grandfather, and he had the misfortune of being awful. After he died, my mother—as mourners are prone to do—reflected glowingly on her father's golf game.

"Your grandfather was a wonderful golfer," she said to me.

My dad, who had played the most with Grandpa, remembered things differently.

---

* Shanks are so feared in golf that most players don't even like to use the word. They're the shots that discharge violently off your club and well to the side of where you were aiming. Once you get the shanks, it's hard to shake them. Trust me, I've had them. They're awful.

"He was terrible," he whispered. "He could never get the ball in the air."

It was only in college that I started to dabble in the game, occasionally stealing off with my roommates on spring afternoons with one set of clubs among us. We would drive twenty minutes off campus to play a dinky nine-hole course named Rockingham, where few holes measured more than three hundred yards, where there were only a handful of trees, and where even in my earliest tear-up-the-turf days as a golfer, it was hard not to break 50.

You could get around Rockingham in little more than an hour, so one April afternoon in our senior year, still groggy from whatever damage we had incurred the night before, we agreed we'd sneak in a round before dark. Until then the Masters was on TV, and Greg Norman had a six-shot lead, so we settled into the couches of our grungy apartment, nursed our hangovers, and prepared to watch the man nicknamed the Great White Shark cruise to his first green jacket.

I had no particular attachment to Greg Norman or really any golfer at that point. But Norman was an inviting figure—chiseled and confident, with an unabashed swagger—and I had paid enough attention to golf to know that the Masters was something that had narrowly eluded him for years. I was looking forward to seeing him finally break through—right up until the point it was apparent he wouldn't.

It's probably strange to admit that the moment that truly sold me on golf was one defined by someone else's misery. We all have a dark side, I suppose. But the enjoyment for me was not so much derived from Norman's collapse. In fact, if at one point we thought we were going to wait until after the CBS telecast to head to the golf course, we eventually deemed his public writhing too painful to witness. When Norman splashed his tee shot in the water on the par-3 sixteenth, all but assuring the Masters title for Nick Faldo, we decided we'd had enough; my roommate Sully clicked the TV off in disgust, and four of us filed out the door and headed to Rockingham. I was disappointed for Norman, but I remained fascinated, my head spinning like when you walk out of a movie filled with so many plot twists you need to confirm with others everything that happened.

Until then I was unaware golf could do that. It didn't occur to me that the golf swing was essentially a living organism that could get up and leave you at a time of its own choosing, or that someone who had navigated a course so skillfully one moment could flail helplessly the next.

But that, I learned later, was Greg Norman. There were times when he appeared unflappable, looking, as Dan Jenkins wrote in *Golf Digest*, "like the guy you send out to kill James Bond." You wouldn't cast a character like Norman—broad shouldered and blond, with that Australian accent—to play the victim. And yet on so many occasions even prior to that Sunday, he was.

To say no golfer lost more than Norman is imprecise because there are scores of professional golfers who don't even sniff a chance to win major tournaments. Besides, Norman won plenty—ninety times around the world, including two British Opens. Prior to Tiger Woods, his 331 weeks atop the world ranking was a record. We should all be such losers.

Still, if you define losing as standing alluringly close to a prize and failing to capture it, then Norman lost. If losing is when the prevailing emotion afterward is regret, then Norman was in a class of his own.

In 1986, Norman led all four majors heading into the final round, but he won only one, the British Open at Turnberry. In the Masters that year, he had a chance to force a playoff with Jack Nicklaus, but he flared a four iron into the crowd on the eighteenth hole, made bogey, and lost by one. In the PGA Championship, Norman floundered to a 40 on the back nine, then watched as Bob Tway holed out from a bunker for a birdie and the win. The cruel blows continued. Larry Mize miraculously holed out a pitch to beat him in a playoff at the 1987 Masters. Norman lipped out a four-foot putt to lose the 1993 PGA. In 1995, he shot 73 in the final round of the US Open when an even-par 70 would have won.

How could one golfer be so dominant in some spots and so vulnerable in others? The two forces would appear to be diametrically opposed, but there's actually a strong and logical connection. Consider the heights Norman reached with his best golf. He set a record at the Players Championship when he won at 24 under par. In the final round of the 1993 British Open, he shot 64 in blustery conditions. His former instructor Butch Harmon has called that day at Royal St. George's "the best round of golf I've ever seen in my life," and this was said *after* Harmon coached Tiger Woods to eight majors from 1997 to 2002.

In reaching such a rarefied level, however, you risk believing you belong nowhere else. Both of Norman's children describe their father's unwavering confidence, even against the backdrop of disappointment. "Stubbornness runs in our family," his daughter, Morgan-leigh, says. "He's a type A person who believes he's going to succeed more than anyone else."

Says Peter Kostis, a golf analyst for CBS and a leading instructor: "Sometimes that stubbornness gives you the commitment to hit a brilliant shot under pressure. Sometimes it makes you go for a shot you shouldn't try. I saw Greg as having that."

At the far end of confidence is hubris, and as the game's premier player, Norman was arguably ill-prepared for those occasions when things went awry. In recent years Norman has acknowledged that he could have benefited from working with a sports psychologist to better deal with those stressful Sundays.

"During my career, when I first started playing the game, sports psychologists weren't part of your team," he says. "But if I had the ability to trust someone to give me advice or help me with my attitude, damn right I would have been a better player."

What Norman needed help with most was his "contingency management"—knowing how to react when your first plan falls apart. The sports psychologist Jonathan Fader's analogy was knowing to take a different route to work when your usual route is blocked. In Norman's case, he needed to know how to respond when his golf swing began to falter or when a tournament he had control of began to slip from his grasp.

"The idea is you've got to have a plan for when things go wrong and you're faced with challenges," Fader says. "The way I work with people is I say we're preparing for excellence. But you're always going to have unwanted outcomes, so if you're prepared for them, you're going to arrive at the quickest path to recovery."

By the time Norman entered his forties, it was apparent contingency management was a skill he needed. Although the 1996 Masters was his most dramatic collapse—the one that put him on the cover of *Sports Illustrated* crouched over in anguish—he has always maintained that the loss to Mize in 1987 was more devastating. It's the major that had him weeping on the beach outside his Florida home until three the next morning, the one he has said took four full years to get over. The main problem, he said, is that he failed to see it coming. The climactic sequence came on the second playoff hole, the eleventh, with Norman's ball safely on the green and Mize off near the twelfth tee after missing his approach right. One hundred and forty feet away, Mize thought he had to get down in two to have any chance of extending the playoff. Norman was pretty sure he wouldn't. Instead, Mize holed the chip to win outright.

"That's the one that gutted me most because I thought I was in total control," Norman says some three decades later. "And that's something I talked to my kids about. I explained to them if you think you're in total control, expect the unexpected. When everything looks great, look for trouble."

However jaded Norman could have been by his streak of bad luck, he persisted in thinking he was due one climactic breakthrough at the tournament he valued most. "If I have one dream left in golf," Norman said in 1994, "it's to win at Augusta. If I told you different, I'd be lying, not only to you, but to myself."

Two years later in the Masters, Norman shot 63 the first day, then opened up a six-shot lead through fifty-four holes. On the night before the final round, Norman bumped into the esteemed British golf writer Peter Dobereiner in the bathroom at Augusta National.

"Well, Greg, not even you can fuck this up now," Dobereiner said.

But of course he did. If nine years earlier Norman was a helpless observer to Mize's improbable chip-in, his fingerprints were all over the events of April 14, 1996, when he shot 78 to Faldo's 67 and lost by five. To classify it properly, the outcome against Mize was a loss while this was a failure. From a distance heading into that round, Norman again appeared in total control. Since he was a half-dozen strokes clear of his nearest pursuers, many of the Australian writers were busy writing their "Norman Wins" stories before he had even teed off. Frank Williams, Norman's then agent, was so convinced his client would cruise to victory, he had bet $10,000 on Norman to win at fourteen to one odds. Offered a $100,000 buyout on Saturday night, he declined.

"It shows you what great judgment I had," Williams says.

Had Williams and others paid closer attention, they would have noticed that Norman's confidence was waning. To one observer, in fact, the Sunday implosion wasn't a surprise at all. At the beginning of the week, CBS announcer Peter Kostis noticed that Norman was experimenting with a stronger grip on the practice range. A grip change to a golfer is like learning a new language. Simply put, how you hold the club dictates how you swing it, which dictates where the ball goes. On Thursday, Norman appeared to take to the change well when he shot 63 and grabbed his two-shot lead. More complicated was Friday, when Kostis noticed Norman's grip on the club had slightly weakened. The golfer didn't hit the ball as precisely but still shot 69 to increase his lead to four. The odd trend continued in the third round. By Kostis's accounting, Norman's grip was back to where it was before the week began, and he was missing shots to both sides of the fairway. Thanks to his chipping and putting, he still shot 71.

"Were it not for some phenomenal short-game work he could have shot 78 or 80, but as it was, he left the golf course with a six-shot lead," Kostis says. "Everybody thought he was playing better and I saw someone reverting to form who was in trouble. You can't play any golf course with a two-way miss, and especially not Augusta National."

On Saturday night, when walking back to the TV compound, Kostis bumped into a Golf Channel reporter who asked him what he thought of Norman's chances in claiming his first Masters. It was a casual exchange that Kostis thought was off the record, so he said he feared Norman was in for a long day based on his erratic ball-striking in the third round. He didn't think anything of the conversation until he showed up Sunday morning and was accosted by Frank Chirkinian, the executive producer of CBS's golf coverage and a good friend of Norman's.

"Frank yells at me, 'Did you tell the whole world that Greg was going to choke and not win the Masters? Greg wants to put his hands on your throat!'" Kostis recalls.

Only then did Kostis realize that his remarks about Norman's swing had made their way onto the air. That the Masters leader got wind of it and called Chirkinian to complain hours before his tee time spoke to his fragile state of mind.

"I said to Frank, 'If all he's got to do on the most important golf day of his life is call you, he's not in a good place,'" Kostis says.

Twenty years later, Norman doesn't disagree.

"I knew deep down Sunday morning I wasn't feeling great," Norman says. "I was completely off."

His apprehension had to do with more than a grip change. In subsequent years, Norman has said he woke up that morning with a stiff back, which he tried to loosen by going for a long walk in the neighborhood around his rental house. But that, too, was only part of the problem. In the hours before his tee time, Norman tells me he was also grappling with a personal issue that had been pushed to the fore. He didn't want to say what it was, and I was unsuccessful in pressing him. The golfer's life, with three marriages (the first of which ended in a reported $103 million divorce settlement) and a wide-ranging business, has always been complicated. Whatever it was, it was percolating enough that he sensed the day was going to be a struggle, six-shot lead or not.

"Things happen that create what you call white noise, and you need to work to eliminate the white noise from the moment you wake up in the morning," he says. "I wasn't able to do that."

Pointless as it is to try to speculate on what someone might have been preoccupied with on a Sunday morning twenty years ago, it's fair to say one thing Norman was contemplating was winning. As recently as the night prior, he had said all the right things about not getting ahead of himself. But then he was still pressed by reporters on what a win would mean. And there was Dobereiner saying there was no way he could lose. And then Kostis saying he still could . . .

"I imagine he was thinking about the times that he had been beaten that he shouldn't have," Williams says. "If it was me, I'd be thinking, 'I can't fuck this up again.'"

In sports, our relationship with goals can be complicated. As much as we're told to identify specific benchmarks and pursue them, the focus on the end result can be paralyzing. Born from this conflict is the golf cliché "Take it one shot at a time," which, as vapid as it sounds, is a means of steering attention away from a result and toward a process. As the sports psychiatrist Dr. Michael Lardon says, the alternative "is you're just trying as hard as you can to win a tournament, which can get a little overwhelming."

With this in mind, one can begin to see how Norman's six-shot lead was as much a burden as it was a blessing. So much unhealthy focus had been placed on what awaited on the eighteenth green when he shouldn't have looked past the tee shot on number one.

"I wasn't one hundred percent prepared for the responsibility of what I had in front of me," Norman says. "And I said to my kids after, whenever you're in an important situation like that, you have to be so strong that you can compartmentalize all the shit that goes on in your mind. That was one moment I didn't do it, and I paid the price deeply."

It turns out that Harmon had given an interview that morning in which he talked about his student finally being "at peace with himself on this golf course." Yet when Norman arrived for his warm-up session, he was a mess.

"I could feel it," Norman says. "My swing wasn't there, and I said to Butch I was off. And Butch said, 'No, everything looks great.' And I said, 'No, Butch, it's not great. I can feel it.'"

Although Harmon could immediately detect a difference in Norman, he says his objective at that point was to try to soothe the player's nerves. When I mention the "personal issue" that Norman says he was consumed with, Harmon nods knowingly. The two men have never spoken about it, but Harmon says one day he'll get around to asking.

"I've always said one night he and I were going to get drunk somewhere and I was going to say, 'OK, what the fuck happened Sunday?'" Harmon says. "He's never told [caddie Tony Navarro] and I what it was, but we knew something was wrong because we were both standing there saying, 'Who is this guy? This is not the guy who left last night.'"

At that point, you might say Norman's fate was sealed, that doubt needed only to seep in a little before there was a flood of it. But Norman says the day could have been salvaged had he been honest with Harmon and Navarro and told them what was really going on. But he never did, and by the time he missed the first fairway en route to an opening bogey, there was no turning back.

"I should have turned to them both and just purged," he says. "It would have taken ten minutes, and it would have been over with. But I didn't do it. So the lesson there is don't harbor things internally. Don't push the elephant under the rug. Anxiety and happiness both come from within. And so you have to ask, which one do you prefer?"

The collapse was both swift and painstaking, leading *Sports Illustrated*'s Rick Reilly to describe the round as a "4½-hour cringe." Norman's six-shot lead was down to five by the time he walked off the first green. By the time he walked off the eighth, it was three. Then came perhaps the afternoon's most dispiriting sequence, an approach shot to the uphill ninth that landed on the green, then began trickling back down the hill like a pebble off a roof. Another bogey, and the lead was just two. Norman looked like a ghost, glassy-eyed and ashen, as he traversed the back nine. It wasn't just that his commanding Saturday night lead was gone. It was that he was drained of the will to get it back. On the fifteenth hole, after Norman saw a last-gasp eagle chip spin out of the hole, he toppled over in pain. On eighteen, after Faldo holed out for the win and his third Masters title, he wrapped his longtime rival in the type of sympathetic embrace you normally see at wakes. It was all over, and Norman was left to somehow make sense of everything that had just happened.

In this way, he summoned his best performance of the week.

FOR THREE YEARS prior to working at *Golf Digest*, I worked two beats at a newspaper, the New York Rangers and golf, and I was always struck by the contrast in how players in the two sports had to account for losing. In hockey, losing is a given, even on good teams. Teams lose games, and with those losses comes an expectation that you explain yourself—who blew an assignment, what you need to do better. When there was a defenseman who got burned on the winning goal, the press would all dutifully gather around his locker while his teammates unlaced their skates in silence. I doubt hockey players enjoy this process, but even in the depths of losing streaks, with seasons and jobs on the line, it is just part of the deal.

Where golf is different is that the gravitational pull is almost always toward the players playing well, to the extent that you often hear golfers end interviews by saying they hope they get to talk to the press again tomorrow; in other words, they hope to shoot a low enough score to still be deemed interesting. The typical player who posts a couple of 75s, meanwhile, can go through the tournament unnoticed, head home on Friday, and only answer to his caddie and his wife.

The exception in golf has always been the players at the top of the food chain: Jack Nicklaus and Arnold Palmer, Norman and Tiger Woods. They all reached that level, of course, because they worked their way into contention more often than not. But even when they didn't, there were enough microphones in their faces that they had to put words to their disappointment quicker than their peers. The standard for this has always been Nicklaus, who won eighteen majors and finished second in nineteen more and had a knack for handling both outcomes with the same level of grace. When I ask Norman about his model for dealing with losing, he pointed to the player he grew up idolizing in Australia.

"You have to win with humility, and you have to lose with humility," Norman says. "I saw if Jack was able to do it, then I could, too."

Compared to Norman, however, you might say Nicklaus's version of losing was of a nobler variety. For starters, he won so many big tournaments, it was easier to be diplomatic about the ones he didn't. But it also seemed that Nicklaus's losses were often a function of bad timing. He wasn't immune from bad rounds in big spots, but more likely someone just channeled their best golf at his expense, like when Tom Watson shot 65 to his 66 to win the 1977 British Open at Turnberry, or when Watson chipped in at Pebble Beach five years later to edge Nicklaus again. To look at it this way, Nicklaus's most notable disappointments were "losses" as opposed to "failures." Norman certainly experienced some of this as well: in back-to-back Grand Slam events, Tway and Mize executed once-in-a-lifetime shots against him to win their only major. But in the larger context of Norman's career, with so many chances and so few conversions, those losses said something about him, too.

"Sometimes you just get beat even when you play good. You've got no control over that," Harmon, Norman's former coach, says. "With Greg, a lot of times things just happened to him. But a lot he brought on, too."

What made Norman's media appearances Sunday night after his Masters loss so resonant is that he never hid from this reality. There was no talk of a stiff back or a personal issue. He blamed no one but himself.

"I screwed up," Norman told the press. "It's all on me. I know that, but losing the Masters is not the end of the world. I let this one get away, but I still have a pretty good life. I'll wake up tomorrow still breathing, I hope. All these hiccups I have, they must be for a reason. All this is just a test; I just don't know what the test is yet."

The media session was interminable. Norman was asked about his loss in every imaginable way—the poor iron shots, his nerves, his legacy, whether it was all a by-product of his perfectionism. Lost in all this could have been the fact that his opponent, Faldo, shot five under par to win his sixth major. "Even if I had played half-decent, it would have been a good tussle with Nick," Norman said. "Nick played great golf. There's no two ways about it. He played great and I played poor."

Our setbacks tend to blind us to others' successes. I think of being eleven and giving up a walk-off grand slam in Little League, when I could focus only on the pitch I left over the middle of the plate, not the impeccable timing of the kid who hammered it into the parking lot. These are the opportunities to recognize the fault is not solely our own. To venture too far in the other direction is to absolve yourself of any blame. But Norman that evening was able to maintain that difficult balance Dr. Jim Loehr says is so essential: owning up to his mistakes while acknowledging the loss wasn't solely his doing. This isn't just important for making a loss constructive. It's also a tenet of good sportsmanship.

"It's the mark of being a great champion, being able to take your defeats as well as your wins," Norman's caddie, Navarro, says. "I thought Greg did a great job giving Nick Faldo his due. It was not only him saying how we messed up, but that Nick played well and did everything he needed to win. Greg handled it well by looking him in the eye and saying, 'Good on you. You won.'"

As cathartic a moment as it was for Norman, it was enlightening to everyone else. Watching at home was fifteen-year-old Adam Scott, who would succeed Norman as Australian golf's most prominent star. At the time, Scott thought he was merely watching his hero lose a tournament.

What he wouldn't realize until later was how instructive the episode would be when he experienced his own major meltdown at the 2012 British Open at Royal Lytham and St. Annes, where he bogeyed the last four holes to lose by one.

"You could say it was a very similar situation to me at Lytham," Scott tells me. "You know, it's maybe not what you want to do, walk into the media center and face questions about why you didn't execute and why you failed. But I definitely drew on that experience of watching Greg go through it and take it on the chin. I came away with a better understanding of what the game is about, and one thing is that you can't be afraid to lose. You have to put yourself in that position because it's the only way you'll ever win."

What's easy to forget now is the distance Norman traveled to get to that point. Unlike his hero Nicklaus, Norman had long had a strained relationship with the media, with reporters feeling that they knew more about Norman's lifestyle of yachts and private jets than anything he actually felt. He was arrogant but also defensive. The editor in chief of *Golf Digest*, Jerry Tarde, tells a story about writing a column critical of Norman in the early 1990s, in which he referred to Norman as golf's version of Madonna, all style and no substance. Shortly afterward, he and Norman met for a breakfast so tense Tarde thought Norman was about to reach across the table and slug him.

"With the press before that tournament I would say he was very confrontational," his agent Williams says. "If anyone said anything he didn't like, he'd come straight back at them in an aggressive way."

In 1996, however, the result of being exposed in such a cruel light was that Norman for once dropped the pretense. It was different from his earlier losses, perhaps because this was the most precipitous fall yet, or maybe because he was older, forty-one, and he had been building toward this. Plus, there was the simple reality that he had just pissed away the Masters and everyone was there to see it, so there was no sense in trying to hide behind some resilient facade.

"I thought he handled it beautifully," Kostis says. "I think Greg became a better person because of it. He was humbled by it and learned from it, and as a result he became more human to his fans."

Sitting in the scoring hut next to Faldo, Norman thought of players who found a reason to avoid talking at all after such a performance—planes to catch, mysterious injuries that required immediate attention. These examples persist today, golfers ducking out from a difficult situation, then issuing an innocuous statement or tweet hours later.

"I had always despised that," Norman told me of players dodging the press. "Even though I knew I was going to get drilled by people who weren't Greg Norman fans, I respected their professions as journalists. At the end of the day it was my professional code of conduct. Look, there were times when I declined an interview, sure. But at some point you have to face the music. And you can either do it in front of the people with cameras and microphones, or you're going to have to do it looking in the mirror when you're having a shave in the morning."

So Norman bared his soul to the press, and afterward,

he had to tend to the fragile emotions of his traveling party. Everyone was in tears—his daughter, Morgan-leigh; his then wife, Laura; even his agent, Williams, who had seen the $140,000 payday disappear one errant shot at a time. Morgan-leigh was thirteen at the time, and she remembers "watching the emotion circulate through our family," she says. "It was really tough, and yet no matter how hard it was, he was still just our dad trying to make us laugh. I don't remember it from a golf perspective. I just remember looking at him and thinking at the end of the day, he was going to be OK."

If there was an opportunity for Norman to drop his guard, it would have been upon boarding his plane for the ride back to Florida. Instead, seeing the assortment of red eyes staring back at him, he held firm that he would be just fine.

"He came on, and he said, 'Oh, come on, it's just a game,'" Williams recalls. "'Think about all the money I've made from hitting a little white ball from A to B. Think about all the guys who work their tails off in factories. I tell you what we're going to do. We're going to stay on this plane and drink it dry.'

"And so we did," Williams continues. "I'm sure underneath it all he really wanted to lock himself in a room and mourn, but he wanted to make everyone feel better."

FOR THE FIRST seventy-nine years of the Masters, no Australian had won a green jacket, a piece of trivia that was rolled out every April as an opportunity to revisit Norman's many Augusta disasters. That looked to change on a misty Sunday in 2013 when Scott entered the fourth round a shot off the lead. Greg Norman was home in Florida, watching a player he had mentored through the early years of his career. As Scott entered the final holes of his battle with Angel Cabrera, Norman called his son, Gregory, who lived down the road.

"He said, 'Holy shit, he's going to pull this off,'" Gregory recalls. "So I drove over. It was a very intense ending, and when Adam made the final putt to win, we were both in tears."

I ask Gregory if he thinks a piece of his father was wistful that the breakthrough moment belonged to someone else.

"It's a good question," Gregory says. "I think a lesser man would be resentful that someone got what he wanted so badly. But my dad wasn't that way in the slightest. He was overcome with pride and joy."

Norman's happiness appears genuine these days. He is sixty-one, but a remarkably young sixty-one, based not only on his still-impressive physique but also his teenager-like sharing habits on social media. I made particular note of this as I was trying to track Norman down for an interview and he seemed to be taunting me by posting photos from ski slopes and beaches, with the occasional snapshot aboard his jet mixed in.

He plays competitive golf only sparingly these days and instead remains immersed in his business, the Greg Norman Company, which has divisions for clothing, golf course design, and wine, among other things. According to his daughter, who serves as the company's creative director, Norman's energy level rivals that of her toddler son.

"I always tell people when we hire them that this is definitely not a nine-to-five job," Morgan-leigh says. "He's always the first one awake, and he's always thinking about it. You ask him anything about any of our companies and he knows exactly what's going on."

In his post-golf life, Norman has endured his share of setbacks. He cites laying off a portion of his staff during the 2008 financial crisis as the "most stressful thing I've ever done." More recently, he had an abbreviated run as the lead analyst for Fox in its coverage of the US Open, lasting just the 2015 season before the network, underwhelmed by his performance, opted to replace him.

Norman says he felt "completely broadsided" by his dismissal, particularly since he thought he had done a decent job. Nonetheless, it's hard to feel too bad for him. According to *Golf Digest*'s annual ranking of the top earners in golf, he made $12 million in 2015, putting him behind only Nicklaus, Palmer, and Gary Player among former players. It's worth noting that those three each had vastly more successful major-championship careers, which might lead to the conclusion that Norman would be an even richer man today had he gotten the job done better on Sundays. Maybe. But I also think Norman's appeal was wrapped up in the entirety of his biography, the losses included. As I said, I'm not sure I'd have thought much of Norman had he shot even par that Sunday at Augusta and won by three.

But seeing him lose in the way that he did, I was drawn to his vulnerability as much as his talent. And I wasn't alone in thinking this.

In the lead-up to Norman's return to Augusta for the 1997 Masters, my colleague at *Golf Digest* Mike Stachura visited the player's office in Jupiter, Florida, to sift through the more than eight thousand pieces of mail Norman received after his collapse against Faldo. The letters came from world leaders (President George H. W. Bush: "You did more for the game of golf in defeat than you have done in victory"), from fellow tour players (Scott Hoch, who missed his own short putt that would have won the 1990 Masters: "We know what you are going through"), and from kids (ten-year-old David Tiffenberg: "We can't always have our heart's desire, but failing can make us stronger"). Even the mother of Larry Mize, the man who stole the 1987 Masters from right under Norman's feet, wrote to pass on her condolences. In the years since, the letters have kept coming. Norman says he has "tens of thousands" in boxes in his home, and though the messages vary, they're all born from the same connection.

"It's very simple," Norman tells me. "I stood up and embraced the failure of it all. I accepted the fact that one of the most precious things in my whole life, I didn't get. And in that situation, it really hit home with people."

The 2016 Masters marked the twenty-year anniversary of Norman's collapse against Faldo, which is noteworthy when you consider how both tournaments ended. The 2016 tournament was where defending champion Jordan Spieth had a five-shot lead with nine holes to play on Sunday before he confronted his own Norman-like disaster on the twelfth hole, dunking two balls in the water and making a quadruple-bogey 7. He lost the lead, never recovered, and the green jacket went to the unheralded Englishman Danny Willett instead. I was there to see the whole thing, and in some ways it was a more painful sequence than what Norman endured. While Norman's loss was a slow bleed over the course of an afternoon, Spieth's tournament unraveled in just a couple of swings. Even worse, as the previous year's winner, Spieth was compelled to stick around to slip the coveted jacket on Willett's shoulders, then clap and smile as the new champion posed for the cameras.

When Spieth stood before the press in the gloaming moments later, his eyes were red, his voice quivering.

"As you can imagine, I can't think of anybody else who may have had a tougher ceremony to experience," Spieth said. "It was very tough given that it's so soon after the finish."

When Norman and I spoke, he had twenty years to put words to his disappointment, but Spieth was freshly removed from the most devastating finish of his career. He was twenty-two, and already had a Masters and a US Open title to his name, but there was now a question of the type of scar tissue this loss would leave. A definitive answer won't be available for some time, especially with so much of his career still in front of him. But in the immediate aftermath at least, Spieth followed the example set by Norman in speaking to the episode honestly.

"Big picture, this will hurt," he said. "It will take a while."

While there's a lot that Spieth can probably glean from Norman's experience in blowing the Masters, their shared setback is fairly unique. Most of us don't lose on national TV, and we don't usually have our private plane waiting on the tarmac ready to cart us out of town.

But at a certain level, heartbreak is universal, and here's where Norman's story is still valuable not just to Jordan Spieth but to the rest of us as well. However crushed Norman was by his loss at Augusta, he's never sought to gloss over the experience. Over time it became the event that reinforced to him the value of humility and helped fuel the success he's achieved in his post-golf career. Among his frequent social media postings is what Norman calls his "Monday Motivator," very often a picture from his playing career accompanied by an inspirational quote. Not surprisingly, a favorite topic is failure and how one often needs to be dragged through the darkness to have a better appreciation of the light.

"The question of success will be decided by your own level of commitment," Norman has said. "That's what makes failure so great. You can't really appreciate success—I mean *really* appreciate it—until you've failed. So let's get after it."

3

Pride and Perspective: What Michael Dukakis Gained When He Didn't Gain the White House

Pride is the mask of one's own faults.
—JEWISH PROVERB

NOT EVERYONE I reached out to wanted to talk to me. I sent notes to Jim Kelly, the losing quarterback of four straight Super Bowls with the Buffalo Bills, but got nowhere. Same thing with Bill Buckner, the Boston Red Sox first baseman who in 1986 famously allowed a ball to trickle through his legs to let the Mets win the World Series. I imagined Buckner reading my plaintive email at his kitchen table, muttering something dismissively, then hitting the delete button. Or maybe it went into his spam folder. Either way, I never heard back.

When I called Ralph Branca, who gave up the "Shot Heard 'Round the World" to Bobby Thomson in 1951, I got the former Brooklyn Dodgers pitcher on the first ring and had to start right in with my pitch. This book is about losing, and—"*I* didn't lose," Branca said. I audibled: "No, of course you didn't," I said. "I mean, you did, but that's not what I meant. . . ." It went on like that for a few minutes, and Branca eventually conceded my point. But I could tell his heart wasn't in it. I chose not to persist.

I hope you know my objective has never been to denigrate these people but rather the opposite: I want to hold them up as inspiration for the rest of us who lose or fail in countless ways but do so in relative anonymity. But I understood their reluctance (and in some cases refusal) to revisit these episodes. Bill Buckner, for instance, played baseball for twenty-two seasons. He collected twenty-seven hundred hits, won a batting title, and played in an All-Star Game. Yet here I was, the latest in an endless line of people reducing his career to one play in one game on a chilly Saturday night in October 1986. I'm not sure I'd always want to relive my colossal screwup, either.

Without the benefit of hearing from them directly, it's difficult for me to know exactly how Buckner and others look back at these moments that have been seared into the public consciousness. I know they haven't shied from the topic completely, so maybe it's no big deal. Perhaps I reached out at the wrong time or they just missed the message, and they'd otherwise be open to discussing their failures at length. But I also wonder how much now, even decades later, they have to contend with the intervention of pride.

It's an elusive concept, pride. When we're kids, we think of pride as only a good thing. We take pride in our work. Parents look at their children with pride. It is the pride I take in my home that compels me to trim the hedges and mow my modest patch of lawn. These are instances in which pride propels us forward in a manner that is beneficial both to society and ourselves.

But we're told pride can be dangerous, too, that it leads to a fixation on oneself that can be counterproductive. It places too great an emphasis on how things *look*. I heard an interview with the actor Jason Bateman recently, who admitted he turned down good roles because he thought they were too small for him. "Pride gets in the way of a lot of good decisions," he said on Marc Maron's *WTF* podcast.

"There are two forms of pride in psychology," Stanford University psychology professor Carol Dweck tells me. "One is very natural, a pride in achievement. You went for something and succeeded. And then there's a pride when you just feel better than others. 'I got a better grade. I make more money. I have a better spouse.'"

This is the kind of pride that, in a biblical context, is considered a sin. It's what leads to hubris and a blindness to one's limitations. When I asked the rabbi Marc Gellman about pride, he quoted the proverb, "Pride goeth before a fall," which is another way of saying overconfidence often comes at a price. The greater our estimation of ourselves, the more we consider ourselves immune from everyday struggles, the less we think we need the guidance and protection of a higher being. Think about the times we throw out our backs when attempting to lift too much weight, or when we drive around aimlessly because we refuse to stop and ask for directions. Even the most inconsequential of setbacks can be the result of an inflated sense of self.

"The highest virtue in the Bible is humility," Rabbi Gellman tells me. "When Moses dies, and he had accomplished more than any other human being—my God, he had emancipated an entire people from Egypt—the Bible's description of him is that he was the most humble of men."

"And the opposite of that is essentially pretending you're God."

As Gellman says, to understand the perils of pride, you first need to consider all the things that you're not doing. You're *not* addressing your weaknesses. You're *not* open to hearing about ways you can be better. A surplus of pride was how Greg Norman dug himself a hole in so many of golf's biggest tournaments.

Again, I don't profess to know the prism through which Bill Buckner or Jim Kelly view their losses. But I do know the people I've talked to who have moved on from disappointment do so because pride is one thing they've been able to suppress.

You don't have to believe in God to appreciate the trappings of pride. In her influential book, *Mindset: The New Psychology of Success*, Dr. Carol Dweck theorizes that people are owners of either a "growth" or a "fixed" mindset. The distinction is between those who see their abilities as something that can be developed and those who feel that talent and intelligence are innate. On the humility-pride spectrum, you might say it's the difference between people who see the merits of learning from their mistakes and those who don't see the point.

Dweck's most celebrated study involved administering a set of tests to a group of fifth graders, half of whom were praised for their intelligence, the other half for their effort. The difference in approach had residual effects on the children in subsequent tests: The "effort" kids came to embrace the challenge of learning even as the tests grew more difficult; the "smart" kids grew frustrated when their superior intelligence failed them. One group had displayed a "growth" mindset; the other, a "fixed."

"Children with the fixed mindset want to make sure they succeed. Smart people should always succeed," Dweck writes. "But for children with the growth mindset, success is about stretching themselves. It's about becoming smarter."

A growth mindset sees the benefits in being tested, even if it doesn't always lead to success. It prepares you to weather disappointment. A growth mindset is Reshma Saujani throwing herself into another bold venture in the wake of two humbling political losses. Although I didn't have the proper name for it then, I suppose you can say this book started with my struggle to teach my kids a growth mindset—how losing should be viewed as less an eventuality and more an opportunity. "People in a growth mindset don't just *seek* challenge, they thrive on it," Dweck writes.

So you can see how the growth mindset is an admirable goal. But it's worth asking whether the mindset is within everyone's grasp. Aren't some people just wired to

ointment better than others? Maybe, but the
ven Southwick and Dennis Charney have de-
t's a skill that can be developed. In studying
pment of resilience in people ranging from former
Vietnam War POWs to victims of sexual abuse, they arrived
at ten "resilience factors" common among those who were
able to effectively deal with stress and trauma. In their book,
Resilience: The Science of Mastering Life's Greatest Challenges,
Southwick and Charney list the factors as "realistic optimism, facing fear, moral compass, religion and spirituality,
social support, resilient role models, physical fitness, brain
fitness, cognitive and emotional flexibility, and meaning and
purpose." You'll notice these resilience factors are reliant less
on innate traits and more on our choices. "Fortunately, to
withstand, overcome and grow from these experiences, we
don't need to have superior genes," Southwick and Charney
write. "But we do need to prepare ourselves."*

Carol Dweck acknowledges we are all wired differently
to start. But our makeups—what we might be born with—
and our mindsets are two different things, and the whole
point of a growth mindset is recognizing that we have the
biggest say in how we approach our problems.

"This growth mindset is based on the belief that your
basic qualities are things you can cultivate through your ef-

---

* Martin Seligman, the director of the Positive Psychology Center at the University
of Pennsylvania, has arrived at similar findings about the development of resilience.
Seligman's term for how we process challenges is our "explanatory style." Like
Dweck, he says some people explain challenges as impossible to avoid and they feel
helpless in their ability to address them, while others view them as fleeting problems they have the power to improve.

forts," Dweck writes. "Although people may differ in every which way in their initial talents and aptitudes, interests, or temperaments, everyone can change and grow through application and experience."

In Dweck's view, a growth mindset doesn't guarantee your failings will springboard you into success, but it does mean you learn to appreciate, and even benefit from, the process. And that means that even if subjected to the most public and humiliating of defeats, you can emerge with your dignity intact.

If anyone would know something about this, it would be a man who ran for president and came up well short of the White House.

I REACH MICHAEL Dukakis in his office at Northeastern University. He is in his early eighties, and it's the height of summer, but his schedule is still jammed, so much so that toward the end of our conversation he announces he has to cut out pretty soon to "go downtown and talk to some people about billboards." I'm not exactly sure what that means, but it sounds important.

It's been three decades since Dukakis was the Democratic nominee for president in 1988, and to answer your question, yes, of course he still wishes he'd won. At no point does he suggest otherwise. By all accounts, Dukakis's life post-politics has been meaningful and content. But only a master of political spin would try to tell you things worked out for the better having lost.

"You don't run for president to lose," he says.

And Dukakis didn't just lose by a little. The Massachusetts governor claimed 46 percent of the popular vote, but he was trounced in the electoral college, capturing only 111 delegates against George H. W. Bush's 426. It was never even close, which is made even more remarkable considering how far *ahead* Dukakis was in the polls earlier that summer.

The collection of men who have been a major party's nominee for president constitute an exclusive club, and truth be told, there are plenty in that group more outwardly exciting than Michael Dukakis. This goes at least a little way toward explaining why he lost. In the heart of his campaign, Dukakis was remarkably even-keeled, his voice rising and lowering at the appropriate times in his stump speech, but otherwise he laid out his vision in the way you might talk about cleaning your gutters.

That might sound like an insult, but there's a compliment in there, too, because Dukakis never got ahead of himself. He remained committed to the process. At the peak of his campaign, when he emerged from the Democratic convention with a 17 percent lead in the polls, Dukakis didn't, in the words of his son, John, "spend much time picking out the drapes in the White House." And when he saw his lead frittered away over the course of that fall, he simply committed himself to clawing his way back.

"My dad is a steady guy," John says. "His highs aren't too high, and his lows are never too low. Sometimes that was read as being boring. But there's something about being tenacious and incredibly energetic, and using that energy in a way that sustains you. So if you're in the Super Bowl, you're not the guy who jumps offside on the first couple of downs because you're so excited."

Somewhere in this depiction of Michael Dukakis lies the paradox of his career. He was never the most electric candidate, a trait best exemplified when he allowed his opponent to dictate the conversation in the election's most pivotal hours. It was the absence of the stereotypical political ego that might have cost Dukakis the presidency. But it also helps explain why he was able to lead a purposeful existence long after his presidential dreams had passed.

DUKAKIS SAYS HE owes his career in politics to his freshman year at Swarthmore, where he arrived with the intention of being a pre-med but was stumped by an introductory physics class. After experiencing only success in high school—an exemplary student, he also ran the Boston Marathon at seventeen in a respectable 3:30—it was a jarring and unprecedented setback.

"For the first time in my life I just couldn't get it," he says. "I got a charitable D, and it wasn't because I didn't work hard. I just couldn't figure it out. I had always done well with this kind of stuff, but over time you're going to have these defeats, and it should at least give you the experience of not always succeeding. In that sense, it was good training."

Much of Dukakis's resilience can be traced to his parents, Greek immigrants whose American dream story was often cited during his campaigns. Dukakis's father, Panos, arrived in the United States at fifteen without any money and not knowing a lick of English, but he worked his way through school. He graduated from Harvard Medical School by twenty-seven and went on to practice medicine in Brookline for fifty-two years. Dukakis says his mother was the first Greek American woman to go away to college and enjoyed a long career as a schoolteacher.

"In terms of role models and whatever it did for me genetically, I was really blessed," Dukakis says. "I had a couple of parents who were extraordinary."

The persistence displayed by his parents has never been far from Dukakis's mind. It's what helped fuel his desire to serve the country that had granted them opportunity, and it's what helped temper the disappointments that were inevitable in a life in politics. What also helped is he was an unabashed optimist, persistent in his faith that a better solution was within reach. "He'll take a loss and move on from it and ask, 'What can I learn from it?'" his daughter, Andrea, says. "I wish I were more like him."

Dukakis's most crushing defeat actually came a decade before he lost the presidency. Certainly 1988 was the election he was best known for losing and the one he lost by the more disheartening margin. But the presidential election was always an uphill march, even when he was ahead in the polls. Ten years earlier, however, Dukakis was a forty-four-year-old incumbent governor relishing what he thought was tangible progress from his first term in office. It was an election he should have won and that most polls said he was poised to win with ease, which is why his subsequent loss in the Democratic primary was such a crushing, unforeseen blow.

"That was a huge defeat," Dukakis says. "I thought we were doing good things. I had inherited a state that was in terrible shape economically, and I felt like we were coming back. We thought this one was going to be easy, and it turned out there's no such thing."

The temptation would be to look at Dukakis's career and say the lost governor's race in 1978 couldn't have been that bad given he won the job back four years later, which is true: Dukakis *did* recover. The thing is, at the time, he didn't know that. In fact, he thought his career in politics was over. One of the hardest things about losing is that in the direct wake, everything can appear so horribly bleak— like waking up with a pounding headache and, for a moment, fearing it'll be there for the rest of your life. Dukakis didn't know his successor, Ed King, would end up bungling his time in office, opening the door for Dukakis to win back the governorship in 1982 and again in 1986. He didn't know that his star would rise so quickly in the party that he would win the nomination to run against Vice President Bush. Dukakis just thought he would go down as a one-term governor who had fumbled away a life in public office.

"Quite frankly I did not think I was going to run again," he says.

The primary election that year was such a nonevent in the Dukakis family that his son, John, didn't bother to come home from California as he normally would for a big election. But then came word that his father had lost, and John hopped on a red-eye. When he returned home, he says, Michael was ashen.

"He looked like he had been punched in the gut a few times," John says.

Andrea Dukakis's recollection was of her father lying in bed, covered in a quilt, unable to grasp what had happened. Shortly after the primary, the Dukakis family went on a previously scheduled trip to Nantucket. It rained the entire time. Pictures showed them all draped in raincoats.

"It was emblematic of how we all felt," Andrea says.

ONE OF DWECK'S observations of fixed mindsets is they tend to shy away from resistance. If there's a chance of failure, they'd rather not even try. I see this with Charlie, my oldest. He likes to *know* he's good at an endeavor before he throws himself into it.

By Dweck's theory, fixed mindsets seek validation of their superiority, and they're leery of anything that exposes otherwise. She tells the story of a French chef who committed suicide when he became consumed by the prospect of a lower rating in the newest Michelin Guide of European restaurants. Never mind that the lower rating never materialized, or that even if it did, it would present an opportunity to improve upon it. The mere threat of inferiority was devastating.

"People who believe in fixed traits feel an urgency to

succeed, and when they do, they may feel more than pride. They may feel a sense of superiority, since success means that their fixed traits are better than other people's," Dweck writes in *Mindset*. "However, lurking behind that self-esteem of the fixed mindset is a simple question: If you're *somebody* when you're successful, what are you when you're unsuccessful?"

Had Michael Dukakis been of a fixed mindset, there's no way he'd have run for office again in the wake of his primary loss in 1978. A fixed mindset would have taken stock of the landscape in front of him and perhaps determined the system was rigged. And he couldn't have borne the idea of throwing himself into another campaign and losing. It would have been too much. Best to just practice law.

But Dukakis, perhaps recalling the example of a father who came to this country speaking only Greek and still put himself through Harvard, didn't view the world that way. Whatever thoughts he had about the end of his political career subsided with time. His wallowing period lasted until his term expired, but then he had to get a job, eventually landing at Harvard's John F. Kennedy School of Government. He found teaching a natural outlet for his inclination for service, and it enabled him to stay up on—and occasionally in—the news. And one of the apparent things was that his successor, King, was doing a lousy job, his tenure marred by corruption in his administration. Here is where luck played a part. Had King delivered as governor, Dukakis might have considered a different career path. He had only wanted to be governor of Massachusetts. No other job in politics really mattered to him, and it turned out to be the man who disrupted that dream who inadvertently revived it.

"Had he done a reasonably decent job, it's highly unlikely King could have been beaten for reelection. Fortunately for me he didn't do a very good job," Dukakis says. "It was a sleazy administration with a lot of corruption. And it was only because of that people started coming to me and saying you really ought to take another shot. So I decided to do it. But believe me, there was no overconfidence this time."

Losing is the ultimate truth serum because it forces you to confront your weaknesses head-on. It wasn't just that Dukakis won when he ran for governor again in 1982. He ended up being a much better governor. He was more inclusive, a better consensus builder. Looking back at his first stint, he realized he arrogantly tried to jam policy through whether he had buy-in from legislators or not. The second time, humbled by defeat, he saw the importance of seeking their input from the start, which led to results.

"I became a much better listener, which is a much more important quality to have if you're going to be an effective leader," Dukakis says. "I began understanding that as a governor you can bring people together who don't like each other, and because you're the governor, you can sit them down to work together and achieve great things."

"As hard as it was at the time, it helped him a great deal," John Dukakis says of his father. "He wouldn't have been as strong, and opportunities wouldn't have presented themselves had he not gone through that loss."

Under Dukakis, his state experienced what became known as the "Massachusetts Miracle," an economic turnaround that included an influx of technology-related jobs, a dramatic drop in unemployment, and a cut in taxes. In 1986, he was named the most effective governor in the United States by the National Governors Association and won reelection with a whopping 69 percent of the vote. The timing, two years out from the next presidential election, was auspicious. Ronald Reagan's term was ending, and the Democratic Party needed someone who could rally its middle-class base. What better person than a principled, highly efficient son of immigrants who had just turned around his home state?

DUKAKIS HAD TO be sold on running for president. Fresh off his successful reelection, he was prepared to build on the momentum of the previous four years, so to look beyond that required some coaxing. Days after the 1986 election, his top aide, John Sasso, handed him a memo outlining a case for a Dukakis candidacy—jobs, development, budgetary discipline. Plus, Washington was a mess. The Reagan administration was awash in the Iran-Contra scandal, which painted the current president as out of touch, at best. Dukakis's supporters convinced him he could do better.

"His whole life was about being governor, but he ran

for president because he thought he could do best for the country," Andrea Dukakis says.

Speaking of humility versus pride, you could make the case there is nothing humble about running for president. It is an exercise in narcissism—the speeches, the commercials, the endless fund-raisers in which your theme in so many words is, *I'm way better than the next guy*. No doubt, Dukakis had supreme confidence in his abilities, and when he entered the Democratic race, he did so because he thought he could make the type of difference nationwide that he had made at home. Is that pride? Probably. But in Dukakis's case, the arrogance of anointing himself the answer to the country's problems was offset by the fact that he genuinely wanted to serve. The chest-beating was merely a means to an end. And considering what he subjected himself to over the course of his campaign, his pride proved to be one thing that never got in the way.

Broadly, Dukakis's presidential campaign could be divided into three parts. There was the early outsider stage when, as a little-known governor, he was fortunate to finish third in Iowa. There was the rewarding middle part when, thanks to his campaign's momentum and the trouble besetting his opponents, he seized the Democratic nomination and a lead in the general election polls. And there was the last part when the Bush campaign identified a strategy of ripping Dukakis to shreds, and he failed to summon a meaningful response.

This wasn't the *only* reason Dukakis lost. Bush was vice president to a still-popular president and had his own extensive background as an ambassador and as head of the CIA. In the final days of the Cold War, there remained valid questions about Dukakis's foreign policy credentials. Plus, attacks from Bush or not, Dukakis lacked fire. He was too levelheaded. The word used to describe him was "technocrat," which to this day I rarely see in a non–Michael Dukakis context. In one of the 1988 campaign's seminal moments, CNN's Bernard Shaw challenged Dukakis's stance against capital punishment in a debate by asking how he'd respond if it were his wife, Kitty, who was raped and murdered. Dukakis answered calmly and dispassionately— the topic might as well have been taxes—and said it wouldn't change his mind. From an outside perspective, his response raised a fair question: If that couldn't get him going, what the hell could?

The answer was not much, and heaven knows the Bush campaign tried. With the vice president flailing, Bush's top aide, Lee Atwater, turned the campaign into a referendum on all things wrong with the Democrats' guy. There were insinuations that Dukakis had chronic depression (he didn't). They seized on Dukakis's nuanced stance about the Pledge of Allegiance (as governor, Dukakis vetoed a bill that would impose fines on teachers who did not lead their classes in the pledge). But no strategy was more impactful than the one involving a criminal named Willie Horton.

As governor, Dukakis had supported a weekend furlough program for inmates as part of their rehabilitation. In one instance, Horton, a convicted murderer, was released on a furlough and went on a crime spree that included assault, armed robbery, and rape in Maryland. Never mind that Dukakis actually didn't start the furlough program (although he did choose to uphold it). The way the Bush campaign framed it, Dukakis may as well have been driving Horton's getaway car. A Republican group released a now-infamous commercial that highlighted the Horton story and sought to prey on the basest of suburban fears: If you vote for Michael Dukakis, there will be a pack of criminals terrorizing your neighborhood soon. Decades later, the Horton ad still nags at Dukakis, not so much because of how misleading it was but because he failed to say anything about it.

"I mean this Willie Horton thing, hell, the most liberal furlough program in 1988 was the Reagan-Bush furlough program in the federal prison system. I never said that," Dukakis tells me. "In fact, I don't think Bush even knew they *had* a furlough program. But, you know, if they're going to come at you, and you're not going to say that, in retrospect, it's pretty dumb."

And that wasn't the case with just the Horton incident. The Republicans took shot after shot at Dukakis, and the candidate barely said a word. Another favorite target was Dukakis's thin national security record, which his campaign sought to counter with a visit to a defense contractor and a photo op of Dukakis aboard the most advanced tank in the military's arsenal. But the event was a farce. The five-foot-eight Dukakis looked like a kid riding the Zamboni between periods of a hockey game. The oversized helmet he wore was ripe for caricature, and the Bush campaign jumped on it, producing a TV spot that sought to show how overmatched the governor was on matters of defense. Again, it worked. A former Dukakis campaign staffer, Josh King, has written at length about the tank debacle, including how the phrase "Dukakis in a tank" has become synonymous with any political event gone awry. In his book, *Off Script: An Advance Man's Guide to White House Stagecraft, Campaign Spectacle, and Political Suicide*, King describes how the Bush campaign immediately recognized the episode as a gift.

"We literally convulsed with laughter because it completely undercut, visually, any credibility Dukakis had as commander in chief," Bush deputy campaign manager Rich Bond told King. "He looked ridiculous. You could tell he was a fish out of water, that he was very uncomfortable."

Already on the defensive, Dukakis's advisers hoped his ride aboard the tank would be occasion to change the perception of the candidate. It would instead become known, in King's words, as "the worst political event in history."

THE FIXED MINDSET response to all this is to say that Dukakis never stood a chance. By many accounts, the 1988 presidential campaign was one of the most vicious in history and opened the door for the steady flow of personal attacks that have become the norm in American politics today. If Dukakis wanted to find someone to blame for his resounding loss that November, he could have picked any number of Bush staffers, if not members of his own campaign for failing to shield him from ridicule. The fact that he didn't* spoke to his character; the problem was his to solve.

In *Mindset,* Dweck points to tennis great John McEnroe as an athlete who was quick to assign blame to outside factors—umpires, court conditions, even, in one famous instance, a TV cameraman whose headset he could overhear during the French Open. Anyone familiar with McEnroe's repertoire of tossed rackets and tirades at line officials probably isn't surprised by this. McEnroe was awesomely talented but lacked the maturity and discipline to persist when his career hit a rough patch. That's a fixed mindset— when things go south on you, you react as if there's nothing you can do. The tournament when the cameraman's headset distracted him was the 1984 French Open, when he blew a two-set lead over Ivan Lendl and lost. McEnroe never seriously contended in the tournament again.

Unlike with McEnroe, Dukakis recognized that the failures of his campaign ultimately fell to him. He tells me that, just as he's told dozens of interviewers who've asked what went wrong in his bid for the country's highest office. The point isn't that Bush fought dirty. It's that Dukakis failed to fight dirty back.

"The mistake was not having a carefully thought-out strategy for dealing with the attacks from the beginning,

---

* Days before the general election, CBS's Dan Rather pressed Dukakis on who was responsible for the tank idea. The anchor put the question to the candidate twice, and Dukakis initially refused to answer. Eventually he relented by insisting it was his decision. "Michael Dukakis put me in," he said.

preferably one that turned it into a character review of the guy who was doing it. It's something I had done the second time around against Ed King, so it's not like I hadn't been through this," he says. "In my case it was clearly my responsibility, and I made the decision that ultimately contributed to my defeat."

A fair question at this point is, *why?* Why didn't Dukakis fire back? You might say it was principle, that he thought the campaign was above such petty sniping. Candidates say this sort of thing all the time. "The American people want to talk about the issues," and so on. And that's partially true. Dukakis *did* think that's what the public wanted. He thought he was taking not only the nobler road but also the road that would curry favor with voters. But he was wrong. Because the more time he spent defending himself about the Pledge of Allegiance or Willie Horton or whatever the Bush campaign was lobbing out there that day, the less time he could talk about *his* plan and *his* vision. To use a hockey analogy, you can't score any goals if you can't get the puck out of your own zone.

In our conversation, I remark to Dukakis that history has not looked favorably at the Bush campaign. Most vividly, a 2008 documentary, *Boogie Man*, paints an unflattering picture of Lee Atwater's aggressive tactics and views Dukakis sympathetically. "So which is better?" I ask. "Is it better to be right and lose, or be wrong and win?"

Dukakis pauses before he answers.

"Well, I don't like the latter, but I don't like the former, either," he says. "I mean, I'm a guy who has a certain amount of integrity to him, and beliefs, and if you start compromising those values and those beliefs in an effort to try to win, what do you have left?

"But then again, I wasn't running to lose."

Right until the end, Dukakis held out hope for victory. He had managed a bit of a rally in the fall and thought there were a couple of key states that could turn his way. This was a pre-Internet era, so there was not an endless Twitter stream of exit polls reminding him how futile his efforts were. And a candidate and his family, in the words of Andrea Dukakis, are "in the eye of the hurricane," always hustling from one event to the next without much of an opportunity to take stock of their surroundings. Dukakis did TV interviews with local affiliates in key states straight through until 7:30 election night. Only then did he look up and realize there would be no relocation to 1600 Pennsylvania Avenue.

"It was a difficult night," John Dukakis says. "We were with people who had worked for a solid year and a half of one-hundred-hour weeks. It was pretty sad because here was the realization that this wasn't going to happen. But he kept his game face. He was steady as he usually is."

I had always heard that politicians prepare two speeches on election night, one for a win, the other if they lose. But Dukakis says that wasn't the case for him. He's always been more of an extemporaneous speaker, jotting down a few talking points but otherwise winging it.

As concession speeches go, his was noteworthy considering everything he had just endured. It wasn't the place for settling scores, but you could understand if he merely offered some platitudes, thanked his supporters, and headed on his way. Yet even as someone who had just experienced the worst side of politics, Dukakis chose to emphasize everything the field still had to offer.

"There is nothing you can do in this world more fulfilling and more satisfying than giving of yourself to others and making a contribution to your community and your state and your nation and your fellow citizens," Dukakis said. "I don't want you to be discouraged. I want you to be encouraged by what you've done in this campaign. I hope many of you will go into politics and public service. It is a noble profession."

The governor went on to talk about his father and the responsibility that comes with living in a country that can offer so much to people who often arrive with so little. After months of pumping himself up, Dukakis's humility was still intact. He was just a cog in a machine that had mostly churned in his favor.

I ask Dukakis what we can glean from his speech that night, why he remained so committed to a profession that at that point had let him down. His response speaks to the importance of seeing the bigger picture. Sometimes the easiest way to process a loss is to be grateful for all the other times you've won.

"Look, I've had an incredible life," he tells me. "Here I am, this Greek kid from Brookline, Mass. I'm a governor of my state three times and my party's nominee for the presidency. You can't have this kind of life and blame the system."

SHORTLY AFTER HIS defeat on election night, Dukakis had a conversation with Walter Mondale, who four years earlier had lost to Ronald Reagan by an even more decisive margin. The subject was moving on, and Mondale relayed the question he had posed to another losing Democratic nominee, George McGovern.

"When did you get over this?" Mondale had asked McGovern.

At that point it was sixteen years since McGovern lost to Richard Nixon. McGovern responded, "When I do, I'll let you know."

There are two types of getting over a loss, really. I think of it as a sting followed by an ache. Earlier I told you about the bad pass I made in a state playoff hockey game that contributed to the end of our high school season. When the game was over, I walked outside to the parking lot and threw my varsity jacket into a puddle. That was me feeling the sting. Eventually I got on the bus and was able to laugh about it with my friends. But the ache would last for years.

The morning after the election, Dukakis woke up, dismissed his Secret Service detail, and rode the T to work. He was still the governor of Massachusetts, and the state required his attention. A day later he headed out to buy groceries on foot alone.

"Dad, where are you going?" Andrea recalls asking him.

He answered as if he wasn't just recently shadowed by men with guns. "I'm going to the supermarket."

Dukakis's way of dealing with the sting was a return to normalcy. But the ache lasted with him, too. To Dukakis, the presidency wasn't about riding in Air Force One or putting up guests in the Lincoln Bedroom. Rather, the job was his best chance to make the most difference, and he lived with the regret not only over the four years of his opponent's term but also over the subsequent presidency of Bush's son. "If I had beaten the old man," he likes to say, "you never would have heard of the kid." He's kidding only to an extent.

"You don't understand, guys like me, we love pressure. We want to be making decisions," he says. "We don't like sitting on the sidelines watching other people make decisions that we think are not in the public interest. That's why you go into politics. So no, I've never thought that it was a good thing for me to lose."

Dukakis's commitment to service is why, in the words of his son, John, "he never thought of politics as a dirty word." It's why he wrote, alongside the late Illinois senator Paul Simon, the book *How to Get into Politics—and Why.* And it's why after leaving the governor's office in 1991, he dove into life as a college professor, with stints at the University of Hawaii, UCLA, Florida Atlantic University, and Northeastern University. It's a life he wouldn't have known had he made it to the White House, but he attacks it with equal vigor, even at eighty-one blocking out hours of his schedule to meet individually with students. Outside of teaching, he has become devoted to the cause of creating a rail link between Boston's North and South stations.

"He's so passionate about empowering other people to make sure their voices are heard," says Christina Warriner, Dukakis's former student assistant at Northeastern. "I know he wanted to make a change nationally, but he sees the difference he can make in the life he leads now."

Given the breadth of Dukakis's accomplishments, you wonder if it burns him that his legacy is so tied to the failures of 1988. The rape question, Willie Horton, that stupid tank—all risk undermining decades of good work, but when I ask Dukakis if he resents his portrayal as a caricature, he said that's the cost of doing business.

"Look, if you go into politics, don't be surprised if there are at least some people who go at you critically," he tells me. "That's part of life, and you've got to be able to handle it."

A pragmatist above all, Dukakis recognizes that being known for something is still better than nothing. Had he only been a three-term governor of Massachusetts, his platform would have been smaller, and he wouldn't have the same opportunity to advance the causes that matter to him. If he had to endure a few jokes on late-night TV at his expense, so be it.

"I think he has a gift, which I wish I had, in that he really doesn't care," John says. "I don't think those things bedevil him in the least. My dad's legacy in the kind of ways that he cares about is intact. He's willing to accept what's out there because in the end he did some good things and he's a good man, and that's a pretty important thing to say."

There is perhaps no better example of a growth mindset than someone who runs for president, loses badly, and still sees the merits in the experience. What else are you preparing for if not the most important job in the world? But if Dukakis was able to see a campaign as a stop on a larger journey, the rest of us might be wise to follow suit.

In some form or another, there's always a new race to run.

4

The "Why Bother?" Point: Susan Lucci's Real-Life Soap Opera

The only way to prove you're a good sport is to lose.
—Ernie Banks

Sportswriters are notorious dabblers in amateur psychology (emphasis on the word "amateur"). You spend enough time in losing locker rooms, or waxing on about one's internal struggle to sink a five-foot putt, and you feel as though you have a decent understanding of how the mind works. In fact, what writing this book has reinforced to me is how little I knew.

In reading and consulting with psychologists over the course of many months, I learned a great deal, but to be honest, I was starting from a pretty modest baseline. In the early stages of my research I didn't know about "contingency management" or "fixed and growth mindsets" or all the other fancy clinical terms that helped shape my understanding of the ways we process loss. My rudimentary thinking started with something I call the "Why bother?" point, which will never pass muster in a PhD program. It is a subjective theory. Still, I feel it adequately describes that familiar by-product of losing in which we get so disheartened we simply withdraw.

Think about how some people seem to embrace the steepest of challenges—completing an Ironman, starting a business, whittling down to a size 6. We all know these people. You might even be one of them. The more daunting the task for them, the more worthwhile the effort. For those who possess the proper growth mindset, "Why bother?" isn't a question they often ask. They are resilient. They have a high tolerance for disappointment. Take Michael Dukakis throwing himself back into the governor's race four years after losing the job; he admirably kept his "Why bother?" point at bay.

But we also know people who tread cautiously and anxiously, and who can't enter into an endeavor without conducting a crude calculation: Is this going to be hard? Will I be any good at it? And *why would I bother* if not? The greater your aversion to failure, the less willing you are to even engage, which we can all agree is a rather limiting mindset.

There was a team in Charlie's hockey league last year that had two brothers who were exceptional. The first three times we played them, we lost by a dispiriting margin— 10–2, 8–1, something like that—with the two brothers scoring almost all of their goals. By the fourth game, the other coaches and I devised a strategy to try to shut them down. We'd clog the middle, keep a third forward high, all in hopes of curtailing their speed up the ice. The plan was generally a success. Our kids played great. Midway through the second period, we were down 2–1. Late in the third, we were still only down two. And when the game was over and we had lost by a respectable 4–1, the other coaches and I were practically ecstatic.

Or at least I thought we should be, but then I entered the locker room. I had a whole bit planned about the character we showed and how a couple of bad bounces were the only difference—which was true. Even in a losing effort, I felt it was one of our best games of the year, which I guess is a difficult concept for a ten-year-old to wrap his head around. Once I started in, I realized no one wanted to hear it. The boys were all furiously unlacing their skates and ripping off their shin guards, no one even looking up other than to toss balled-up pieces of tape in the garbage.

"Hey," I said. "What's the matter with you guys?"

Silence.

"Charlie," I said in the direction of my son. "What is it?"

Only then did Charlie look up. He blew the hair out of his eyes, looked around the room to make sure he had a consensus, then returned his gaze to me.

"I don't know why we have to play these guys," he finally said. "All we ever do is lose."

To reach the "Why bother?" point is to be blind to an upside. It is to build up all kinds of frustration without knowing what to do with it. Consider a direr example. A 2016 report of the 7.4 million Americans out of work revealed seven percent of those people were no longer even looking for jobs. According to the Bureau of Labor Statistics, these are "discouraged workers" who are not currently looking for jobs because "they believe that there are no jobs available for them." A related study led by Princeton University economist Alan Krueger revealed that people who have been unemployed for more than six months have only a one in ten chance of landing a new job in a given year, the stigma of unemployment often a barrier in itself.

"They apply for job after job and are turned down," Krueger tells me. "This process is discouraging and demoralizing to many. It is like being turned down on date after date. . . . Of course, some people are resilient and eventually land new jobs, but a large fraction end up becoming discouraged and stop looking for work."

So many people giving up on their job searches is an extreme example of "Why bother?" thinking, but a sadly common one in a changing economy. Suppose you've answered dozens of online job postings. You've sent out dozens of résumés, and you've checked your email so often you've come to resent any correspondence that is not directly tied to prospective employment. At some point the process becomes draining enough that you'd rather abandon it altogether.

Jeff Bradley was near that point. He had been a sportswriter for more than two decades when he was laid off in 2012 from his position as a baseball writer for New Jersey's *Newark Star-Ledger*. I didn't know Jeff personally, but I knew his work well, and it was always quite good. Prior to covering the Yankees for the *Star-Ledger*, he was a writer for *ESPN the Magazine* with a number of compelling cover stories to his credit. But as advertising revenue and readership plummeted at media outlets around the country, Jeff was deemed expendable, as countless talented journalists have been in recent years. I had lost track of him until recently when I learned he was working as a locker-room attendant at a country club in New Jersey. It was a humbling position for a guy who had often been face-to-face with the superstars of sports, but Jeff didn't care. In searching for other jobs, he told me, he had sent out résumés and cover letters by the bunch but rarely heard back. When he applied for a low-paying job at the weekly paper in his New Jersey suburb, he wasn't even granted an interview.

According to Krueger, this is the point at which thousands of Americans discontinue their job searches. But Jeff wasn't willing to be one of them. He needed the money, and any job was better than giving up. He spent the summer of 2015 picking up other people's towels and cleaning their shoes but at least he received a paycheck.

"I had twenty-seven straight years of always having a job, so not working was something I couldn't accept," he tells me. "I could sit around and sulk all day and think about, 'Why am I not getting any calls back?' But I couldn't give up my search for a job. I owed that to my family, but I also owed it to myself."

In staving off his "Why bother?" point, Jeff still had to wrestle with an acute sense of inadequacy, or helplessness, whatever the word is for when you throw everything you have at a problem and still come up empty. It's what can happen when you put in for a job you're overqualified for and you still don't hear a peep, or when you play your best game of the season and still lose by three. In the absence of tangible validation, you start to wonder if it's even worth the effort.

Pro athletes have their "Why bother?" moments, too. The golfer Sergio Garcia had played thirty-five major championships without winning one when, in 2007, he stood over an eight-foot putt to capture the British Open at Carnoustie. But the putt only grazed the edge of the cup, and Garcia went on to lose in a playoff to Padraig Harrington. Later when trying to make sense of the loss, Garcia wasn't heartened by coming close, nor did he cite the lessons of the experience. Instead he cryptically made reference to playing against "more than the field"—the implication being that larger forces were at work and he was overmatched. On other occasions, Garcia has lamented not being good enough to win majors, when he actually might be one of the five most talented golfers on the planet.

"Sergio is famous for projecting and not taking responsibility. He uses a lot of denial, as in, 'It's not me, it's you,'" says Dr. Michael Lardon, the psychiatrist who specializes in achieving peak performance and who has worked with a number of professional golfers. "When you use that to optimize your mental state, you don't. What you want to do from a loss is you want to gain as much utility out of it as you can."

At the risk of exceeding my allotment of golf examples,

bear with me for one more. For a time, the golfer whose career trajectory was most similar to Garcia's was Phil Mickelson, who failed to win in his first forty-six major attempts, sometimes in heartbreaking fashion. But this is the same Mickelson who is said to carry the attitude of a defensive back, always able to rebound from a recent mistake in the interest of moving forward. Even in the face of all of those losses, in fact, Mickelson possessed an unyielding belief in himself that bordered on delusion.

In 2001, after he was nipped at the end of the 2001 PGA Championship by the little-known David Toms, Mickelson launched into a monologue about how his goal wasn't to win just one major. "I'm trying to win a bunch of majors," he said.

It was a presumptuous remark for a guy who had fallen flat as often as he had, but it also spoke to Mickelson's resolve. And he turned out to be right. Three years later, Mickelson won his first major at the 2004 Masters, and he's since won five majors in all.

"I've always been somebody, ever since I was a kid, that got motivated by failure, that worked harder because of failure," Mickelson said at the 2015 US Open. "Some people get discouraged by that, and it almost pushes them away. But for me it's been a motivator to continue to work harder and get over that hump."

If we're all forced to consider our shortcomings, some, like Mickelson, are just better at filtering their influence. It's not so much that these people are blessedly lacking in doubt. The people worth studying are those saddled with the most doubt of all but who still find a way to persist. As the story goes, the author Stephen King had his manuscript for *Carrie* rejected by thirty different publishers, leading him to toss it in the trash. If not for his wife fishing it out and insisting he keep trying, he might have ended up just another frustrated writer who didn't want to bother with the repeated string of rejections. In history, the worthwhile examples are endless, from Lincoln to Roosevelt, Einstein to Edison. But they exist in areas you might not even consider, too, a testament to how failure and losing are as commonplace as a headache. And it's funny—when I thought of all the people who have outlasted "Why bother?" moments, I couldn't help but wonder about one woman in particular.

I MEET SUSAN Lucci in a coffee shop in midtown Manhattan. She is closing in on seventy but could pass for two decades younger, and as befitting a soap opera icon, she walks in wearing sunglasses the size of sunflowers and carrying an iPhone with a leopard-print case. I've never been a soap opera guy, but I certainly knew Susan Lucci, less for her longtime portrayal of the tormented Erica Kane on *All My Children* and more because when it came to losing, few people lost as publicly and as prolifically as she did.

You might not think of acting, an art, as a win/lose proposition, but if it is, by most measures Lucci has won. She lives in a sprawling home off Garden City Golf Club on Long Island, has two successful kids, and when our

meeting ends, she calls her driver to wheel around the corner to pick her up.

Still, perhaps no name is more synonymous with losing
than Lucci's, all based on a period when she was nominated
for eighteen Daytime Emmys and lost every time. This was
a thing when I was growing up; I remember it vividly. A
twelve-year-old boy would have no other reason to think
about the Daytime Emmys when they rolled around, but
you would always be aware of whether Susan Lucci had
won, and invariably she hadn't.

Lucci became a meme, a punch line. The Chicago Cubs
were "the Susan Lucci of baseball," but not to be confused
with the Buffalo Bills, who were "the Susan Lucci of football." And it wasn't just sports since Martin Scorsese for a
while was "the Susan Lucci of the Oscars." Meanwhile,
there was a woman who had to reconcile how her entire
existence had been reduced to a snarky metaphor for always
falling short.

"Well, I understood it," Lucci says. "But the first time I
heard it I thought, 'Wow.' I didn't want my name to be associated with something so negative."

When I outline the reason for our meeting, that I have
two boys who struggle with losing and I'm on a mission to
learn from those who have mastered the art, she nods
knowingly as if to say, *You've come to the right place.*

Lucci's first nomination came in 1978, and at the time,
she didn't think much of it because the Daytime Emmys
weren't yet a big deal. So when she lost, she essentially
shrugged her shoulders and thought maybe she'd get an-

other chance—which she did, three years later. And she lost again. The cycle continued year after year. As time passed, Lucci fell victim to expectations. When the nominations would arrive, she would hear from castmates as well as her fans that this was her year, and a part of her started to believe it. After all, she thought, there was no way she could lose *again*.

"I would definitely get my hopes up because I thought the story line was good, and the fans were all saying I should win," she says. "I would get into all the excitement about winning. And then I wouldn't and there'd be disappointment."

Before long, her frustration bubbled over; at one point during a ceremony she slammed her fist on the table when it was announced she was passed over again.

"It was the ninth time that it got to me. I remember being very upset," she says. "I never stormed out. I think it was reported that I stormed out. I didn't do that. But I remember the disappointment really got to me."

This could have been Lucci's "Why bother?" moment, the equivalent of her throwing aside her tennis racket and running into the parking lot. She could have stopped going to the Emmys, or she could have decided that she just didn't care. In fact, part of her defense mechanism was to retreat into a protective shell. The Emmys would arrive, and Lucci and her family would celebrate the nomination, but when it came time for the actual event, she subconsciously tuned out. Those awkward occasions when they stuffed the camera in her face just as they announced someone else had won again—Lucci says she doesn't really remember them. She would always smile, and she insists the smiles were genuine, but mostly she was somewhere else.

"When they announced who won, I'd go numb," she says. "Not intentionally, but it was like my body was protecting me. It was crazy."

Only in private did Lucci allow herself a night to cry out the disappointment of each loss, but even then it was behind closed doors, and only briefly.

"It wasn't pretty," she says. "But it took me about a day. Maybe sometimes just the car ride home."

"And then she'd put her boots back on and get to work," her son, Andreas Huber, says. "That's just the type of person she is. She always tried to be very consistent and professional about it."

Over the years, theories circulated about why Lucci was shut out. Her character was a bit ridiculous, marrying half the fictional town of Pine Valley. There was jealousy within the soap opera world because she was daytime TV's highest-paid actress. Plus, she had a knack for picking the most melodramatic scenes when submitting her reel for the awards, which the writer Thomas O'Neil, in his book on the Emmys, described as "drowning her chances in a tsunami of tears." Lucci heard them all, but she was reluctant to dwell on any one reason.

"I don't know, and I will never know," she says. "I know people were saying it was this reason or that reason, but I couldn't be sure. Occasionally I'd be asked, 'How does it feel to be a loser?' and I'd be like, 'I don't feel like a loser.'

So the best I could do to take away from it was to continue to try to grow, and try to do better, regardless of whether I won."

Lucci's response to her Emmy streak calls to mind Dr. Jim Loehr's distinction between losing and failing, and how often the classification is subject to interpretation. Yes, Lucci lost. She was nominated for an award, and she didn't win. But that, at the time at least, was it. You could hardly call it a failure since she was still an exorbitantly paid actress with scores of fans nationwide. But the losses still registered with her enough that she chose, as Dr. Michael Lardon has described, "to gain utility" from them. The essential ingredient in reviewing these episodes is honesty, and Lucci's way of avoiding her "Why bother?" point was to at least look at her losses constructively.

A small example: As an actress, Lucci's training was to look within when assessing her work. How did she feel? Was she being authentic? It was never about appearances. Yet when forced to review her scenes to submit for awards, Lucci noticed she looked down too much. It was a small tic but an important one in that it disrupted the connection with other actors, as well as the audience.

"After a while I was getting nominated and you'd have to look back at some of your scenes, and you'd see technical things like that," she says. "This tendency to look down came from a character who had a lot going on in her life. But I realized it was a lot better to let the audience in by letting them see your eyes."

In identifying an area of weakness and addressing it,

Lucci was reinforcing her belief in growth and not, as she puts it, "resting on my laurels." "The best you can do is keep growing every day," she says. This is probably the healthiest way to handle losing because it shifts the emphasis away from a concrete result and toward an ongoing *process*. You will hear this word a lot in this book because it speaks to the idea that in everything we confront—from tennis matches to job interviews to Emmy Awards—there are the things we can control and the things we can't. To focus on process instead of results is for a tennis player to concentrate on watching the ball and exhaling with every stroke rather than worrying about winning the point. It's about preparing as best as you can for an exam without fixating on the final grade. The problem is we've become so results oriented, we have a hard time divorcing ourselves from more tangible benchmarks.

"The way society is geared, we care about your grade, about your bank account, about your place on the money list," Dr. Lardon says. "The paradox is that the people who are really successful, they're not thinking about winning and losing or comparison thoughts. They're thinking about the execution of what they can do."

Lucci fell into this category. Of course she wanted to win an Emmy. But the focus was her development as an actress, which hinged on more than the number of statuettes in her living room. Because she began to approach her streak so reasonably, she was able to connect with people in a way she wouldn't have otherwise. Put it another way: If her eighteen losses continued with a string of pouts and slammed fists on the table, no one would care much if she ever won. But because she smiled and applauded and made efforts not to denigrate the winners, her fan base grew. Sure, there were jokes, some of which she was happy to participate in. When she hosted *Saturday Night Live* in 1990, the opening monologue involved the show's cast parading past her with all their Emmys. But Lucci's bad luck also inspired real affection, such as when two sympathetic girls in Pennsylvania sent her their ballet trophies to keep. Or when the documentary filmmaker Randy Stone sent her his Oscar with an attached note reading, "Keep this until you win the Emmy."

When it came to consolations, though, the most rewarding ones came from within the walls of her own home. Lucci's two children, Liza and Andreas, both of whom had taken their father's last name, had grown accustomed to the ritual of their mother shuttling off for the Emmys and coming home empty-handed. Both attempted to soften the blow through poems, cards, and makeshift bouquets, all of which made clear they didn't agree with the actual result. When Lucci was shut out for the fourteenth time, she was greeted at home by Andreas, who assured her all the Emmys she was due would be waiting for her in heaven.

Then one night in May 1999, Andreas was home from college and at a friend's house for a birthday celebration. So low were his family's expectations that he wasn't even paying attention to the Emmys telecast that night; instead he was lingering with friends out on the patio. Then his friend's mother rushed through the door.

"Andreas, you need to come inside now and see this," she said. "Your mother just won an Emmy."

Andreas responded, "You're so full of shit."

It was true. On the nineteenth try, Lucci won. If you watch the YouTube clip now, you can see her incredulous look when her name is announced, as if she thought there was a misunderstanding and she was just waiting for it to be corrected. A long standing ovation ensued, followed by Lucci trying to jam nineteen years of acceptance speeches into one, and then there were all sorts of congratulatory moments. A note from President Clinton. The cover of *People* magazine. The outpouring was sincere, but it was about more than Lucci, or *All My Children*, because much of the attention transcended the insular world of soap operas. Instead the moment was about losing and the sentiment that the people who have lost the most are entitled to the biggest celebrations. It was not unlike the jubilation that accompanied Mickelson's first win at the Masters—which makes sense since he was "the Susan Lucci of golf."

Apparent in the immediate aftermath of Lucci's breakthrough was just how much her Emmy streak had become part of her identity. She had lived through it, endured all the punch lines, and was finally allowed to enjoy the spoils of her win. What wasn't clear until later was how much it influenced those around her.

IN THAT SPRING of 1999, Lucci's son, Andreas, was nineteen, and as it turns out, a promising amateur golfer. In

1997, he had progressed enough to compete in the US Junior Amateur Championship, where he played well in a pairing with a highly touted Australian named Adam Scott and later advanced to the quarterfinals. The showing resulted in new attention from college coaches, including some of the best programs in the country. Stanford, where Tiger Woods played, was a suitor, but Andreas ultimately opted for Georgetown, where he ended up winning the Big East Conference title as a freshman.

Andreas was a competitive kid, a trait he inherited from both his parents (his father, Helmut, grew up a skier and soccer player in Austria). When he talked about his experiences as a young athlete, it all sounded similar to what my boys confront. There were occasions when his emotions took over—throwing clubs, storming off the green, all the usual golf brat stuff. "Until I was more mature, I was throwing a lot of mini-tantrums on the course," he says.

"It took him a while," his mother says. "There's an expression in my business—use it. If there's something going on, try to channel it to where it's useful. Put it on the stage, put it on your work. And if you can't find anything useful, put it away. If Andreas had a shot he wasn't happy with, he had a hard time putting that away, and it had a way of influencing his next shot."

Golf is the ultimate "Why bother?" game in that it is defined by perpetual failure. I'm now about a 12 handicap, which is the best I've ever been, and it means I make maybe a half-dozen pars per round with only the very occasional birdie. In other words, a typical day of golf for me is one in which two-thirds of the time I'm making some sort of dumb mistake that sabotages a decent score. Andreas's good-to-bad golf ratio has always been more favorable, but then the stakes for him have always been higher. Even at fifteen and sixteen, his golf calendar consisted of tournaments around the country on the elite American Junior Golf Association circuit. Then came Georgetown. And then after dabbling for several years on the trading desk at Deutsche Bank, he worked up the nerve to make a go as a pro. At each stage, he learned the pitfalls of letting frustration mount. And while he drew lessons from a wide range of sources, an essential one was from a woman who often left for a sound stage before dawn.

"This whole time she was going through [her streak] I'm maturing and growing, and I'm recognizing the level of perseverance you have to have to get out of bed every day. My mother, in terms of competing, was in a similar position of putting herself out there every day," he says. "Because [acting] is very much like sports. You have to prove yourself every day and continue to get better, otherwise you're going to get left in the dust. So then I started to get it more, her perseverance. Because in golf, you're getting beat down way more than you're feeling like you've won."

As Andreas is talking, Lucci is sitting beside her son and wearing a surprised smile. At this point she is not a soap opera star, but a mother grateful to see she made an impact. "This is the first time I've ever heard him talk about this," she says.

Though Andreas flirted with making it to the highest levels of professional golf, he never quite got over the hump. He didn't survive the first stage of PGA Tour Qualifying School and missed by two shots a chance to play the European Tour. He was even a contestant on the Golf Channel reality show *The Big Break*, where he went in with high ambitions but flamed out in the second episode—an experience he calls "hugely disappointing and a little embarrassing."

All throughout, his parents were there to talk him off the ledge. And as much as he leaned on his father, whose own resilience was forged growing up in Austria during World War II, it was his mother who had the more identifiable experience with losing.

"A lot of the conversations were filled with her saying things like, 'Please, you don't have to tell me,' or 'Believe me, I know how you feel,'" Andreas says. "She can be a pretty feisty little Italian lady. But it was always supportive, never the opposite."

In 2008, Andreas was in San Diego playing a qualifier for the following season's Canadian Tour, and he opened the tournament poorly. When he called home that night, he was despondent, pacing back and forth on a friend's balcony as he laid out his misfortune. It was as much of a "Why bother?" moment as he had experienced in golf, but his mother refused to indulge him.

"I told my mom I was screwed and all that, but she wasn't giving me an inch," Andreas says. "I was going on about how much I sucked. She wouldn't let me get a word in and would only talk about how I had three more rounds to go and I could still do it."

Huber played under par the next two days to at least give himself a chance going into the final round. On a windy, difficult final day, he ended up qualifying for the Canadian Tour by a shot. Only when driving to the airport the next day did the emotions of the tournament take over, and Huber broke into tears.

Once on the Canadian Tour, the learning curve was steep, and Andreas struggled to make any real money. He plodded along for two more seasons, but eventually he decided he would pursue a career elsewhere, less because he was disheartened and more because he had other entrepreneurial opportunities—particularly a mobile app company that still exists today—that were starting to gain traction. He now is immersed in his work, lives in Manhattan, and says he applies the fierce drive he once reserved for golf to running a business. We'll never know if he would have arrived at the same spot had Lucci won on her first Emmy nomination or never won at all. But he maintains that his mother's experience proved instructive in how to handle setbacks, even if it wasn't something she sought to teach explicitly.

"It wasn't so much what I said to him," Lucci contends. "I think you always lead more by example, and in my case, it was about going to the studio the next day, on time and prepared and wanting to do better. It was rarely me saying, 'Take a lesson from me.'"

It is often the case that the most profound lessons are conveyed less by what we say and more by how we live. Lucci's example was about weathering her streak professionally, and even with good humor. It was about showing up for work even as her name became somewhat of a national joke. Although she spared her kids her rawest moments by weeping behind closed doors, she didn't necessarily need to. Losing well isn't about being immune to disappointment. It's about taking that disappointment and putting it to good use.

5

What Goes Up . . . Can Come Back Up Again: Fay Vincent and the Resilience of the Mind

We learn wisdom from failure much more than from success. We often discover what will do by finding out what will not do; and probably he who never made a mistake never made a discovery.
—SAMUEL SMILES

ONE DAY IN December 1956, Fay Vincent lay motionless in a hospital bed in North Adams, Massachusetts, revisiting the decision that changed everything. Alone and frightened, he was preoccupied by a simple yet odd-sounding regret: "I should have peed out the window."

If you're familiar with the name Fay Vincent, you probably remember him as the commissioner of Major League Baseball who presided over the game during a time of particular turbulence. He took over in 1989 in the immediate aftermath of the divisive Pete Rose scandal, which banished the game's all-time hit leader for betting on baseball. There was a historic earthquake that disrupted the World Series; months later, a suspension of the volatile New York Yankees owner George Steinbrenner. After that, there was a showdown with owners that ended up costing Vincent his job.

Decades before, though, Vincent was an eighteen-year-old kid who had broken his back after falling four stories out a window. All, really, because he had to piss and couldn't make it to the bathroom.

When we discuss losing, we often do so in the context of one clearly defined side prevailing over another. This is the losing my boys know best and Vincent has known, too—first as an athlete, later as an attorney, and most prominently as commissioner when the baseball owners decided he no longer represented their interests. But there is also a more nebulous type of losing in which there are no tangible winners. We all experience this in some form or another—a loss of identity, or self, often stemming from the unwelcome encroachment of some new reality. Remember the sportswriter Jeff Bradley who lost his job at a newspaper and went on to work as a locker-room attendant? Among his new challenges was an existence vastly different from what he had known before. These setbacks are born from different origins, but they still carry the same character-building potential as any other loss.

At eighteen, Vincent lost a part of himself. He was in his first year at Williams College, the captain of the freshman football team with a promising future on the varsity. Vincent's father, Fay Sr., had been the captain of the football and baseball teams at Yale, and Fay Jr., too, had defined himself primarily as an athlete. He was six foot three and 230 pounds and played tackle both ways, and while he didn't harbor illusions of a career in the NFL, he anticipated that college would revolve around Saturday afternoon games and fraternity parties that night.

That existence lasted for one autumn. Then came that

December, when Vincent's roommates locked him in his small dorm room as a prank, taking the doorknob with them. When Vincent awoke from a nap, he desperately needed to use the bathroom, so he decided to try to shimmy out his window and through another window to get there. Instead he slipped off the icy ledge. Halfway down, he crashed into a railing that broke two vertebrae in his back. It was the better of two options. Had he fallen directly to the ground, he likely wouldn't have survived.

Regardless, life as Vincent knew it was over. He was finished as an athlete, and it would be months before he could walk, although never again without a noticeable limp.

It was an episode that took mere seconds, and most of us would be satisfied to characterize it as an unfortunate freak accident. Vincent interprets it differently.

"That was a failure," he tells me. "It was an enormous failure of judgment."

When I decided that losing was a topic I wanted to explore for a book, I constructed a list featuring an assortment of athletes, politicians, and businesspeople, with the occasional soap opera star sprinkled in for flavor. In reaching out to friends and colleagues for their suggestions, what I found startling was the volume and breadth of responses. Losing stirs a lot of passions, to the extent that once a week or so I'd get a text urging me to talk to this person or that. Some friends even suggested themselves, which is an odd brand of self-promotion, considering the topic.

The name Fay Vincent wasn't on my radar. I recalled his time in baseball and knew it didn't end well. Beyond that, I hadn't given his story much thought. Only when a mutual friend said the former baseball commissioner often used losing as a theme in commencement speeches at various colleges and prep schools did I email Vincent proposing we meet. He wrote back saying sure and concluding with this: "In my life, I've found failures have led to wisdom while successes can lead to foolish arrogance."

Having been at work on the book for several months by that point, I had long embraced the first part. But it was the second part that reinforced a concept that was still taking shape—that just as we might undersell the benefits of losing, we tend to be blind to the counterproductive effects of winning.

In the NHL, there's a widely held theory that a losing streak is often preceded by a game you were lucky to win. The logic isn't hard to follow. Lucky wins are defined by making all kinds of fundamental mistakes, maybe getting your goalie to bail you out, but still failing to address all the flaws festering below the surface. Then comes the next game, and they're all exposed. In youth sports, it's the same thing. As a hockey coach, our least productive practices are always in the aftermath of wins, the kids so self-satisfied they see no point in toiling through mindless drills. They want to scrimmage or work on breakaway moves, the struggle of the game now superseded by thoughts of how they might celebrate their next goal. I don't blame them. Winning tends to seduce us into thinking we've got it all figured out.

The danger in this way of thinking was embodied by Greg Norman after playing his best golf or by Michael Jordan when he extracted so much pleasure from winning basketball games. Success itself is not the problem. But when success fosters a false sense of invincibility, it is.

"We have a tendency to ascribe success to our own ability or brilliance when it can just be luck or some fortuitous intervention that got us there," Vincent says when I ask him to elaborate on his email response. "With failure we tend to scratch around a long time to come up with a reason."

In his speeches about failure, Vincent lists three in his life that were influential. The first was his "foolish arrogance" in climbing out a fourth-story window. At eighteen, on the heels of an undefeated football season that had just concluded with a win over archrival Amherst, his body was nimble and responsive enough back then that he hadn't even given thought to falling—or at least not until he was tumbling through the air.

"It was the single biggest event of my life," Vincent says. "Every day when I get up I'm reminded of the huge price I've paid, all a function of that one mistake. One day I'm eighteen and I felt I could jump over the moon. Then the next day I was in a hospital bed and I was in rough shape."

Doctors needed to remove two inches of shattered vertebrae, and he would remain in the hospital for six months, eventually being moved to one in Waterbury, Connecticut, to be closer to his family's home. In the process of relearning how to walk, he also had to digest a new reality, and an early transformative moment came when his mother arrived to visit him one day carrying a record of George Gershwin's *Rhapsody in Blue* and a simple message. "She said, 'No matter what happens to you, you'll always be able to enjoy *Rhapsody in Blue*,'" Vincent recalls.

He understood the subtext, and while no one expected a record to heal the wounds of a life-altering injury, it did help open his eyes to the resilience and independence of his mind. "It was all I had left," he says. He would never play football again, but he could read and write and debate. And if he wasn't going to connect with people through athletics, then he'd have to find another way to do it.

IN SPEECHES, VINCENT likes to quote his hero Winston Churchill's own famed commencement address, in which Churchill implored students: "Never give in, never give in, never, never, never, never—in nothing, great or small, large or petty—never give in except to convictions of honor and good sense."

In rallying from political irrelevance to become one of the most celebrated statesmen in history, Churchill has long stood to Vincent and others as a model in perseverance.* But perhaps a closer analogy for Vincent is Churchill's American counterpart Franklin Roosevelt. Like Vincent, Roosevelt seemed to coast through early life. While never

---

* In World War I, Churchill presided over a disastrous invasion of Turkey that resulted in scores of British casualties and his own ouster as first lord of the Admiralty. Decades later, Churchill became a national hero when, as prime minister, he stood in defiance to the Nazis and helped the Allies win World War II.

much of an athlete, he was at least able-bodied, with the
benefits of wealth, good looks, and a bloodline that traced
to the twenty-sixth president of the United States, Teddy
Roosevelt. All these advantages allowed Roosevelt to live
somewhat above the fray, removed from the struggles of
the average American.

Then at thirty-nine, Roosevelt contracted polio, which
paralyzed him below the waist and forced a once gallant
figure to struggle through the daily tasks of getting around
the house and using the bathroom. Of course no one
would choose such an existence, and we can only speculate
whether Roosevelt would have arrived at the same level of
achievement had his body never failed him. What we do
know, though, is that Roosevelt's condition played a direct
role in his rise to the presidency and in his subsequent success. For starters, his public narrative shifted, making the
aloof-seeming Roosevelt not just a sympathetic character,
but one who displayed great determination in the face of
adversity. Internally, it forced Roosevelt to view the challenges facing Americans during the Great Depression with
a degree of empathy he might not have otherwise possessed.

"The particular way in which Roosevelt came back from
his illness exhibited the essential habits of mind and action
that he would deploy during the Great Depression and
World War II: improvisation, experimentation, and perseverance in the face of enormous trouble," the author James
Tobin writes in his book *The Man He Became: How FDR
Defied Polio to Win the Presidency*. "The way he fought
against his paralysis, trying one thing, then another when

the first thing failed, and then a third, was perfectly re-flected in his pragmatic response to the crises of his presidency."

Vincent found himself on a path similar to Roosevelt's in that his accident informed both his view of the world and the world's view of him. As with the thirty-second president, Vincent benefited from a reshaped image in the eyes of his peers. When he returned to school, he was made president of his fraternity, as well as an officer in his class, and as much as he'd like to think these appointments were the by-product of his intelligence and charisma, he couldn't discount that initially, at least, people just felt sorry for him.

"People would say, 'Oh, you deserve great credit for getting through this,' but when it happens, what choice do you have?" he says now. "You can either sit home and suck your thumb and feel sorry for yourself, or you can say there's something you can do."

He started on the road back from his devastating injury by following his instincts from that afternoon listening to Gershwin. Although he was always a decent student, he began to devote himself more seriously to academics, knowing that was all he had left. He took on the extra course load to make up the time he had missed, ended up graduating Phi Beta Kappa, and was accepted into Yale Law School.

Here is where Vincent confronted his next great failure, because as much as he thought entry into one of the country's hallowed institutions would be a victory in itself, he struggled while there and finished near the bottom of his class.

"In my world, academic success was to be expected," he says. "I was always at the top of every class, but I got to Yale Law School and it wasn't that easy for me. That was another big failure."

Looking back, Vincent says his struggles in law school could be traced to a specific academic discipline that he didn't quite grasp until it was too late. "Law school puts a great premium on spotting issues," he says. Students would be given a complicated paragraph filled with more than two dozen torts and then be asked to elaborate on the problems they posed. It was bury-your-head-in-a-book type of work, and Vincent recognized he was better at interacting with others. When he graduated, he figured he was screwed.

"I thought that it was going to be a deterrent, and that I was going to have a much more difficult time as a lawyer because I hadn't been very successful," he said. "I thought the law firms rewarded brilliance in law school, and they do. But what I learned is that brilliance in law school doesn't equate with people skills, salesmanship, the ability to manage people and get along with clients."

These areas Vincent took to naturally, and when he was able to hook on with a law firm out of school, he distinguished himself in ways that had to do with more than just lawyering; he was adept at finding creative solutions to complex problems.

Years passed. On the strength of his savvy and nose for conflict, Vincent rose to become a senior partner at a Washington, DC, firm, which found itself the victim of a massive fraud in which a client, Liberty Equities, inflated its financial statements. Vincent never saw it coming, an oversight he says made him a much more discerning judge of character. Later he went to work at the Securities and Exchange Commission, followed by his friend and former classmate Herb Allen appointing him the president of Columbia Pictures, where Vincent presided over a series of hits including *Tootsie* and *Gandhi* but also the infamous flop *Ishtar*. For a brief time he was an executive vice president at Coca-Cola.

What's remarkable about Vincent's career is that for a while it progressed so rapidly, with just the right number of setbacks to make it interesting. If he had retired at age fifty, he would have gone down as an unquestioned success. The problem was when he landed a dream job as the commissioner of baseball, because then everything began crumbling around his feet.

Vincent owes his spot in baseball to his late friend Bart Giamatti, the dynamic former president of Yale University who left academia for a position as president of the National League. At first Vincent was just an outside adviser to Giamatti, helping him negotiate his contract. But when Giamatti was elected to take over for Peter Ueberroth as commissioner, he suggested Vincent, with his rich experience in law, entertainment, and business, join him as his deputy.

The Giamatti tenure was brief and defined by one name: Pete Rose. Look up Giamatti's time in office, and you'd be hard-pressed to read about him in any other context. Between the time he was elected commissioner in the fall of 1988 and when he died of a massive heart attack the following September, the entire episode unfolded: Giamatti catching wind that Rose was betting on baseball; launching, at Vincent's urging, a thorough investigation into Rose's activity; and ultimately banning the game's most prolific hitter from the game. It was one of the most divisive moments in the game's history. I'm ashamed to admit it now, but when I learned of Giamatti's death at fifty-one just days after he threw my favorite player out of the game, my first reaction was to hope that meant the decision would be reversed.

Instead, Vincent, in taking over for Giamatti, dug in his heels even more, and what's clear even today is the disdain he has for Rose or for anyone who would dare defend him. Some of this is personal, dating back to the time during the investigation that Rose referred to Vincent as a "cripple." But there was also Vincent's loyalty to Giamatti, as well as his own role in overseeing the investigation that led to Rose's demise.

"That was twenty-six years ago, and you can see the entire investigation online," Vincent says. "No one has questioned a single fact. Nothing. I'm proud of that."

The polarizing nature of the Rose decision tested Vincent's resolve as commissioner, and it appeared it would remain the focal point of his first few months in office. But then came a more pressing emergency: an earthquake measuring 6.9 on the Richter scale struck the Bay Area minutes before Game 3 of the World Series at San Francisco's Candlestick Park. Vincent was in a box at field level when the quake struck, and the chaos was unlike anything ever confronted before in American professional sports—officials rushing out of the dugouts to help the crowd, fans streaming to the exits, gaping holes in roads and bridges around the stadium. Sixty-three people died in the area.

Strange as it is to say, the earthquake was Vincent's finest moment as commissioner, which is in no way to suggest that he enjoyed it. But in making most of the right decisions, in projecting calm under stress, he helped the game weather a crisis, postponing the Series just long enough for conditions to be made safe, but insisting it be played soon as a rallying point during tragedy.

"The one thing I always knew was trouble," he says. "The earthquake was trouble. Rose was big trouble. Those were the things I really knew what I was doing. The part that was far more difficult for me was the politics and dealing with the owners."

Vincent's last great failure, and the one for which he is best known, was the abrupt end to his tenure as commissioner. Just as Giamatti was inextricably linked to Rose, Vincent's legacy will forever be tied to a losing battle with baseball's owners. That he most likely was right in this conflict is of small consolation.

"I really wanted to be a successful commissioner, and I wasn't," he says. "I now see I made some mistakes. Some of my judgments were bad. But I also see there were some things I just couldn't do."

In the aftermath of the World Series, when he had built up some capital for his handling of the earthquake, Vincent was afforded a brief window into life as the game's top official, where he liked to note, "no one sits in front of you." The problem is that being baseball commissioner is kind of like being a substitute teacher. There's the vague sense that you're in charge but not enough to really matter. And along the way, Vincent faced plenty of resistance. He pushed through realignment of the National League, moving the Chicago Cubs and St. Louis Cardinals to the NL West against the strong objections of those teams, because he felt it was the right thing for the game. When he took on Yankees owner George Steinbrenner for his dealings with a gambler named Howard Spira, he was marginalized by a coterie of owners who thought Vincent was overstepping his bounds. In hindsight, Vincent learned a lesson about choosing the right battles.

"Because I was in tough shape politically, it was a fight I shouldn't have taken on," he says.

Vincent's real downfall, and the reason he was afforded little latitude, was his unwillingness to placate owners on labor issues. In the early nineties when Vincent was in office, the percolating tension between the players union and the owners could basically be summarized like any other labor dispute: the players wanted to make as much money as they could make, and the owners were resentful of the players' power. Vincent's mistake, if you want to call it that, was that he saw the gray area between them and was insistent that the owners try to meet the union halfway. As commissioner, he saw his mandate as serving in the best interests of fans, and the only thing fans cared about was that the game not be interrupted by labor unrest.

The owners interpreted Vincent's job differently and viewed any efforts to work with the union as a display of weakness. The union head at the time was a man named Donald Fehr, and word got around that Fehr, who lived in Westchester County, would occasionally visit Vincent at his home up the road in Greenwich for meetings (a concession to Vincent's limited mobility from his back injury). By one account, which Vincent acknowledges as true, Fehr even helped Vincent's wife, Valerie, bring in the groceries, reaffirming to the owners what they already suspected: the commissioner was lost.

"He was not a political person. He wouldn't just do whatever it takes to get the owners on his side," says Murray Chass, the longtime national baseball columnist for the *New York Times*, who chronicled Vincent's time in office and has grown close with the former commissioner since. "It's not like he was completely green. He had been around the block in his other jobs. But in this particular case he didn't have the inclination to be political, which others urged him to be. He's just not that type of person."

By 1992, less than three years after taking over following Giamatti's death, Vincent's grip on his job was loosening. With negotiations with the players over a new collective bargaining agreement approaching, the owners wanted simply to break the union and were leery of having Vincent at the table. In September, they passed a resolution expressing a lack of confidence in his leadership and asked for his resignation. "There are a lot of issues that come into play here," Phillies president Bill Giles said at the time. "But the number one thing is that people just don't trust him."

Decades earlier, Vincent's fall was off an icy ledge. Now it was from atop baseball. In both cases, it wasn't entirely clear which part was his fault. Once he hit the ground, though, it didn't really matter.

VINCENT LIVES HALF the year on a quiet, wooded street in New Canaan, Connecticut, his large house preceded by a driveway that could accommodate a dozen cars. At seventy-eight, his mobility has deteriorated to the point where he can barely walk, and when I ring the doorbell, his voice comes crackling through the intercom telling me to walk in. When I enter, Vincent is waiting for me in the front room, his feet up in a recliner, various photographs from his days as commissioner lining the shelves. Among Vincent's favorites is actually one from *after* he was commissioner, when he threw out the first pitch at Shea Stadium in 1993, his abbreviated tenure still awkwardly fresh in everyone's mind.

It turns out everything Vincent was trying to protect against as commissioner played out as he feared in the early nineties. With the owners and players still so far apart, the players went on strike in 1994, and for the first time in the game's history, the World Series was canceled. The national pastime was a mess, but at least Fay Vincent wasn't to blame.

Although Vincent wasn't technically fired as commissioner, it was a classic "you can't fire me, I quit" scenario. He had a powerful lawyer, Brendan Sullivan, who was prepared to argue that the owners did not have the power to remove Vincent from office, and legally, both liked Vincent's chances of winning. In a letter to owners on August 20, 1992, Vincent informed them he would "never resign." But the more he thought about it, the more he knew a victory wouldn't come quick, and it wouldn't be pretty.

"I just thought, 'I don't want to do this,'" Vincent recalls. "'Life is too short. I've got health problems. I've got plenty of money. If they don't want me, why do it?' And so I said, 'I don't have the stomach for it.'"

On September 3, Vincent offered his official resignation, but not without firing a salvo at the owners on his way out the door: "Unfortunately, some want the commissioner to put aside the responsibility to act in the 'best interests of baseball'; some want the commissioner to represent only owners, and to do their bidding in all matters," he wrote. "I haven't done that, and I could not do so, because I accepted the position believing the commissioner has a higher duty and that sometimes decisions have to be made that are not in the interest of some owners."

With Vincent, the resentment toward the owners—and specifically Bud Selig, the Milwaukee Brewers owner, who took over his job—has never been far below the surface. But really the prevailing emotion he felt upon losing his job was embarrassment. I'm not sure I'd feel any different if my ousting was chronicled in every newspaper in the country.

"Nobody likes to leave a public position without at least some light applause," he says. "I was very disappointed and embarrassed. I loved baseball, and I thought I was doing the right thing for the game."

Seated in his recliner, occasionally adjusting his sneakers to help the circulation to his feet, Vincent is able to talk about this episode with the benefit of time and perspective. When I press him on what he feels he did wrong, he maintains his mistake was not in standing up to the owners but in failing to make a more effective argument when he did. A shrewder politician, like Giamatti, could have played the game better, but Vincent refused. His story is similar to Michael Dukakis's in that Dukakis, too, held firm to his principles in his campaign against George H. W. Bush, but that wasn't enough to win over the people that mattered. When I suggest to Vincent that both men could claim some moral higher ground, the former commissioner scoffs.

"It didn't matter that I was right," he says. "My job was to prevent baseball from committing some sort of suicide, and I didn't do it. It's not something I look at as some noble distinction. I still failed."

ONE OF THE effects of Vincent's earlier back injury is it instilled in him a sense of impermanence—that we are all, as he says, "a split second away from oblivion." He had money but he knew that might not last. Same thing with status. It's an unsettling thought for those of us who like to think of one day building on the next. But it can also be liberating. Losing is far less daunting when you don't count on having much in the first place.

"I knew not to place too much emphasis on material things, because it could all be gone in a hurry," he says.

Even during successful times, like when he was running Columbia Pictures, Vincent maintained this perspective. He favored a New Testament verse, "For what shall it profit a man, if he shall gain the whole world, and lose his own soul?" It underscored the same sentiment as when his mother played *Rhapsody in Blue* for him: the interior life will outlast everything else.

In this way, Vincent had prepared himself for failure. If you remember the "resilience factors" the psychiatrists Steven Southwick and Dennis Charney listed as common for those who had successfully withstood adversity, many related to one's mental outlook: realistic optimism, a moral and spiritual compass, brain fitness, cognitive flexibility, and an ability to face your fears. Vincent had all of these. In the aftermath of his back injury, he had learned to be fearless and adaptive, had sought guidance from his Jesuit upbringing, and had remained intellectually curious. Whether consciously or not, he had spent years fortifying his protective armor.

"It was a mindset that was very important to me when things were going well, and it was certainly helpful when I wasn't successful. I was reminded that no one is really *that* important," he says. "Now, do I have an ego? Do I have the ability to lose track of my importance? I'm sure I do. But I came to understand that every hill that goes up also comes down."

Upon leaving office, Vincent had an immediate distraction thanks to his back, which required surgery after years of neglect. So the first month out of baseball, just when he would have been seated in the front row of the World Series between Toronto and Atlanta, was spent in a hospital. Once he had recovered, though, he followed through on a bold plan: to rent a house on the river Thames in England and decompress from the stress of the previous few years.

"I figured I'll go over for six months, and when I go to a pub, nobody will know me or say, 'Hey, you're Fay Vincent, why aren't you in baseball?'" he says. "It gave me time to realize there's a new life out there, and there's millions of people in England who've never heard of me or Bud Selig or Pete Rose. So I rented a lovely house, spent six months there, and it was a totally wonderful break."

In the quarter century since leaving baseball, Vincent has been in semiretirement. He's sat on a handful of boards and served briefly as president of the New England Collegiate Baseball League, but otherwise he has spent time refining the narrative of his failures. It's a story he welcomes telling, in part because it's a way to alter the perception that his ouster as commissioner brought only disappointment. As with Greg Norman after blowing the Masters or Michael Dukakis after losing the election, he wants people to know the aftermath of his defeat brought growth in addition to pain. It's evidence of the type of transparency he values in himself as well as in others.

"He's the most honorable man I've met on the management side of baseball," the writer Murray Chass says.

"Even the fact that his telephone numbers are in the telephone directory says something. You don't find too many people in his position who allow their telephone number to be published. But when he was commissioner, he was more approachable than any other commissioner. He's just a straightforward guy."

Since it's fair to assume most of the college graduates Vincent has addressed won't become commissioner of Major League Baseball—or, for that matter, fall out a fourth-floor window—I ask Vincent what the universal lessons are that he passes on to audiences.

His first point is to remind students that to fail is to be in good company. "Failure is a huge part of American, if not human, existence," he says. "Nobody can construct a life in which they're not going to fail." He cites the great historical examples of men and women who have emerged from earlier setbacks to achieve great success. Churchill is one. Another is Ulysses S. Grant, who was so downtrodden he was selling wood at the start of the Civil War, but who eventually took over to lead the Union army to victory and then become the eighteenth president of the United States.

From there Vincent has asked students to look inward. "I say think about your earliest papers. The one you remember is the one you got the worst grade on. You don't remember the one you did really well on. You remember the one you got back from the teacher that said, 'This is unacceptable.' That failure can lead to a commitment not to let that happen again."

He likes to tell the story of a graduation speech he gave

once at the Canterbury School in Connecticut, in which he revisited his laundry list of regrettable moments. A mother approached him afterward.

"She said, 'I'm so glad you did that because our kid didn't do very well here and he thinks he's a failure, but he saw how you failed and that it can be OK,'" Vincent recalls. "That was great. I always say, it's not about whether you fail but whether you learned anything from it. The test of life isn't whether you've fallen, but whether you used the failure to build something that's more concrete and more beneficial."

As with all these stories, Vincent couldn't have immediately appreciated the profound effect his injury at eighteen would have on his life, how it made him more cautious and more introspective, but also better equipped for the challenges he faced later on. It's hard for me to call it a gift since I'm not the one who has struggled to walk for most of my life. Vincent doesn't use that word, either. But in an ironic way, the episode that nearly crippled him is also what made him stronger. If you rise from a fall once, you become that much more confident you can rise again.

6

The Power of Rewriting: How Dan Jansen Revised His Own Script

*The greatest discovery of my generation is that a human being
can alter his life by altering his attitudes of mind.*
—WILLIAM JAMES

THE EASIEST VERSION of Dan Jansen's story, the one that could fit on a business card, is that his life changed with a race one minute and twelve seconds long. It was the 1994 Winter Olympics, and Jansen won the speed skating 1,000-meter race in a world-record 1:12:43. That was the great turning point. That was when he went from Dan Jansen, heartbreak kid, to Dan Jansen, gold medalist, public speaker, inspiration for TV movies and books.

This isn't just my interpretation of his career. Even Jansen acknowledges how easily he could have fallen on the wrong side of history.

"Without that 1:12, I would have been labeled one of the greatest chokers of all time," he says.

Without it, Jansen is there with Bill Buckner and Greg Norman, athletes who let a few bungled moments overshadow otherwise stellar bodies of work. But because he managed to stay upright on a speed skating oval one February day in Norway in 1994, Jansen was allowed a reprieve. He won a gold medal, and for that reason, everything about his story would be different.

So what can Dan Jansen teach us about losing? Haven't the last two decades of his life been spent basking in a storybook win? Curiously, that's the part of his story often misunderstood. For all the doors his Olympic victory opened for him, Jansen says it was everything that came before that shaped him most profoundly. It's a strange thing to say, but by February 1994, the greatest gains had already been made.

"There's no doubt I got more out of losing," Jansen says. "Losing is what teaches you who you are."

JANSEN GREW UP the youngest of nine siblings outside Milwaukee in West Allis, Wisconsin, the son of a police officer and a nurse. West Allis is a rare speed skating hotbed, one of the few towns in the country that boasts a 400-meter skating oval, and each of Dan's older brothers and sisters were active in the sport at one point. Jansen's brother Mike was good enough to represent the United States internationally on World Cup and world championship teams. Dan's brother Dick qualified for the Olympic trials when he was working night shifts as a cop.

There has long been debate over how birth order affects an athlete's growth, including the suggestion that later-born children are more likely to be superior competitors.

The theory is that the younger kids get tossed into competitive environments with the older ones and thus are tested in ways they wouldn't be if confined to their peer group. I should mention that the science on this is inconclusive, and there will always be exceptions to the rule. My older brother is ten years older than I am and such a better tennis player that the only thing I really developed playing against him was an acute sense of my inadequacy.

For the more athletically gifted, however, older siblings can be part of the complex recipe that propels them to the highest level. Cooper Manning, two years older than his brother Peyton and seven years older than the youngest, Eli, tells me it was his brothers' early experiences with backyard competitions that helped lay the foundation for their careers as NFL quarterbacks.

"Even two years is a lot for kids," says Cooper, who played college football at Ole Miss before an injury cut short his athletic career. "It just seems that the older brother has just enough of an edge, and [in the Mannings' case] that had a lot to do with Peyton's competitiveness and fiery work ethic. It probably made him a little craftier and a little more callous."

The former NHL star Chris Drury, who at twelve was also the star of a team that won the Little League World Series, describes a similar dynamic, saying his older brothers were instrumental in keeping him grounded at a time when he was otherwise plenty successful.

"If I wanted an inch against them, I had to grind like crazy," says Drury, whose older brother Ted also played in the NHL. "And there were times when I was a sore loser and they'd call me on it. They'd be like, 'Relax, you're eight. I'm fourteen. This is supposed to happen.'"

This was Jansen's experience as well. He immersed himself in skating at a young age, so much that at ten years old, he and brothers Mike and Dick would make the two-mile run to the rink with a skate in each hand, work out hard for more than an hour, then run the two miles home. And yet no matter how much potential he displayed at a young age, it was tempered by his modest standing within his family.

"You do become more resilient at a young age because you're just trying to keep up with your brothers and sisters," he says. "But half the time you can't, and almost all the time you're not going to win because they're bigger and stronger. So you just keep going. You just try again."

One of the hardest things to do as a sports parent is to teach your kids to work hard without placing too great an emphasis on results. It sounds simple when you type it out like that, but I struggle with it all the time. By all accounts, Jansen's father, Harry, struck the right balance with his kids. If Dan and his brothers were running four miles a night just to get to skating practice, then the sport was more than just an adolescent diversion. But Harry Jansen had a gift for teaching his kids the merits of effort without pressuring them in the process.

"It all goes back to our dad," says Mike Jansen, Dan's older brother by eighteen months. "He just wanted us to do our best and the results were what they were. And he made sure we stayed humble regardless."

When Dan was twelve, he and Mike qualified for the national championships in their respective age groups. Dan was pretty sure he could win and spent most of the car ride to Saint Paul, Minnesota, anticipating his ascent to stardom. But he didn't win. He lost narrowly in his division, and Mike won his. Rather than be happy for his older brother, Dan spent most of the six-hour car ride in tears. When they returned home, Jansen prepared for his father to sit him down and offer some sort of consolation.

"He always had a way of making things better, and so when we finally sat down to talk, I thought it was going to be the greatest thing ever," Dan recalls.

Instead, his dad said, "You know, Dan, there's more to life than skating around in a circle."

That was it. Harry soon left the room, and though he initially left his son confused, the message got through. Dan was permitted to put everything he had into skating, but skating couldn't be all that was in Dan.

Jansen would play other sports—baseball all through high school and a little bit of football—but it soon became clear that his future was on the ice. At sixteen, he set a junior world record in the 500 meters, and two years later, he qualified for the 1984 Olympics in Sarajevo. The experience of those first Olympic Games was all that really mattered to Jansen, and he entered them with minimal expectations. Yet he somehow finished fourth in the 500, missing out on a medal by a mere sixteen-hundredths of a second. Jansen was thrilled. Of course he wanted a medal, but at that point, all he could think was he was eighteen, and he had finished *near* the top, and that was pretty good.

On his way home to West Allis, Jansen was certain the rest of the town shared in his excitement. He privately wondered if a parade was planned. But there wasn't. In fact, when Jansen returned to the United States, the prevailing sentiment was one of sympathy, as in, *Too bad. Better luck next time.*

"It was a learning experience," Jansen says. "I guess I didn't realize at the time how people watching from their living room looked at it all. . . . Maybe because we're Americans and we're a powerhouse, we just win. I mean, they all meant well. And they said, 'Nice try.' But I didn't get a whole lot of congratulations. Not that that's what I was after, but what I didn't realize until then was that [my lack of a medal] was actually disappointing to some people."

The reaction to Jansen's first Olympics reflects a challenge that extends beyond sports in which our emphasis on success overlooks the simple merits of effort and experience. We spend so much time applauding the people who win, we tend to neglect the people who finished back in the pack but sacrificed just as much of themselves. Whether it's the Olympics or a job interview, or even tryouts for the school play, there are rewards for the also-rans that still exist: banking of experience, insight into underlying weaknesses, motivation to do better next time.

This misguided assumption that anyone who doesn't win has only disappointment to show for it is captured in a Jerry Seinfeld stand-up bit about the Olympics. He jokes that the silver medal comes with the implication of failure. "They don't lose by much in these short races, three-hundredths of a second, two-hundredths of a second," Seinfeld says. "I don't know how they live with that, the rest of their lives. Because you got to tell the story. Everyone wants to hear the story. Wow, congratulations, silver medal. Did you trip? Did you not hear the gun go off? Tell us, what happened?"

Jansen's experience after Sarajevo, without a medal of any kind, was consistent with Seinfeld's observation. Unless you're intimately involved, most Olympic sports exist in obscurity, and even when pushed into the spotlight every four years, most of the attention is lavished on the winners. Everyone else is either anonymous or a letdown. The athletes themselves know it's more complicated than that, and as Jansen proved at eighteen, their level of satisfaction depends largely on their expectations.

There's actually some science to this. The psychologists Victoria Medvec, Thomas Gilovich, and Scott Madey studied Olympic athletes on the medal stand at the 1992 Summer Games in Barcelona, asking their undergraduate students to give the athletes' expressions a rating between 1 (miserable) and 10 (euphoric). The gold medalists' expressions were rated the happiest, for obvious reasons. But what's interesting is that the bronze medalists' faces on average rated more than two points higher than those who won silver. This might be surprising since they technically fared worse in the competition, but when you factor in something called "counterfactual thinking," the result actually makes sense.

Psychologists define counterfactual thinking as focusing on what might have been as opposed to what actually happened. It can work for or against you. Imagine you're one of those Olympians on the medal stand. If you've just won a silver medal, you're probably thinking about how you *could* have won gold but are now destined to a lifetime that Seinfeld describes, retelling the same story of everything that went wrong. When you win bronze, however, you've likely contemplated the possibility of winning no medal at all, which makes the one you've got feel pretty good.

We are all prone to counterfactual thinking—in thinking about the jobs we could have landed or the homes we could have owned, but also in sports. I played tennis recently against a guy who is twenty years older than I and thirty pounds overweight. I won in straight sets, but both sets were ugly. I made all kinds of mistakes, smashed my racket against the fence a couple times in frustration, and barely squeaked by him. In my mind, I should have won with ease, and because I didn't, I was exasperated. By contrast, I played another match that same week against a far superior player. I lost, but because it was a respectable showing and I wasn't blown off the court—which I anticipated—I walked away satisfied. That's counterfactual thinking at work. Your expectations can mean the difference between lamenting that you should have done better or being thrilled for faring better than you thought you would.

Jansen's experience in 1984 was his version of a tennis match against a far superior opponent. It was an example of how counterfactual thinking can help. In his mind, the al-

ternative to his fourth-place finish was dead last—or perhaps, because all his buddies were now freshmen in college,
a seat in some tedious university lecture. He wrote in his
memoir that the Sarajevo Games were his only pure Olympics because he went with "low expectations and high principles." The problem is how those expectations would rise
as he ventured further into his skating career, because it
also heightened the prospect of disappointment. Dan
would confront plenty of heartache in the years to come.
And it wasn't just because of what happened on the ice.

ONE WORD I'VE sought to avoid using in this book is
"tragedy" because tragedy denotes something else entirely.
I've worked my entire career in sports, and abuse of the word
there is epidemic. Not giving the ball to Marshawn Lynch
at the goal line in the final seconds of the Super Bowl was a
tragedy. The New York Rangers not winning a Stanley Cup
with Henrik Lundqvist would be a *tragedy*. Neither of these
scenarios remotely meets the definition, and one needs to
scroll the front page of any news website these days to appreciate the difference. Sometimes, though, real tragedy
infiltrates the sports world, and in the most public of ways,
this is what happened with Dan Jansen.

Of the nine Jansen kids, Jane Beres was the third youngest. She was five years older than Dan, but those two, along
with Mike, were grouped together as "the young kids," a
tight subset within an already tight family. "Jane was easily
the most sensitive Jansen, the one most attuned to other

people's feelings and most vulnerable to criticism from the outside," Dan writes in his memoir, *Full Circle*. "I'm like Jane in a lot of respects in that I'm sensitive to the way people feel about me, although I try not to show it."

By 1987, Dan was enjoying the transition from a promising up-and-comer to one of the best skaters in the world, his measurement of success no longer just holding his own but winning. It's important to note that Jansen has always been a competitive guy. He might have digested failure better than others because his family had infused him with perspective, but his objective was no different from every other elite athlete. Skating was paramount, and as he bounced around the globe for various races, he was consumed by the efficiency of his stride and whatever else stood between him and another personal best time.

Then Dan came home to Wisconsin from a World Cup meet to find out Jane, just six days after giving birth to her third daughter, had been diagnosed with leukemia.

"My heart sank. Just sank," Jansen wrote in his memoir. "To that point in my life I hadn't known real tragedy."

Jane's illness was devastating to the entire family, forcing them all to recalibrate their lives. In Dan's case, it wasn't that his sister's condition had halted his career, because he continued to compete after her diagnosis, and even win. But everything now seemed so fleeting, like building a sand castle you knew would be toppled by the next big wave.

Over the ensuing months, as Jansen built toward the 1988 Olympics in Calgary and Jane underwent various transplants and treatments, Dan was forced to confront the reality of his world opening up right as his sister's was closing. He tried to do his part by offering to donate his bone marrow, but a recent bout of mononucleosis was a complicating factor. Plus his family was leery of the disruption it would cause at such a pivotal moment in his skating career. His sister Joanne ended up being the better match for Jane anyway, but Dan was insistent he would have contributed in any way he could.

Just a week before the start of the Olympics, the World Speed Skating Championships happened to be in West Allis and Jansen, at twenty-two, won his first world title. He went to the hospital directly from the rink to show Jane his medal, where she beamed with excitement and they tried to ignore the dark reality of her condition. It would be the last time he saw his sister.

THERE COMES A period fairly early in a skater's development when falling ceases to be a legitimate concern. It happens sometimes but usually only as a consequence of speed, or an overly aggressive turn. Or in the case of Dan Jansen, when your sister dies on the morning of your Olympic race.

On February 14, 1988, the day that Jansen's story became known to the rest of the world, Dan was awakened in the Olympic Village in Calgary by a call from his family asking him to say good-bye to his sister. Jane was on the other end of the line, Mike holding the phone to her ear. She was too weak to speak, so Dan did all the talking. The skater has only a vague memory of what he said, but he does remember asking his mother when she came on the line if he should just pack up and come home. Knowing Jane wanted him to skate, the family agreed that he should stay. Dan still wasn't sure. Less than three hours later, his sister was gone.

Sometimes in sports or elsewhere, an outside traumatic event can serve as a helpful distraction, or even inspiration. The golfer Ben Crenshaw won the Masters just days after burying his beloved teacher and mentor Harvey Penick. In 2010, the British jazz singer Cleo Laine performed a concert hours after the death of her husband, saxophonist John Dankworth. Both Crenshaw and Laine said they felt the departed with them. But Jansen didn't feel Jane in that way. He only felt that he shouldn't be in skates, staring at an empty sheet of ice in front of him.

In accounts of his 500-meter race later that day, there are references to Jansen's blank expression, his face devoid of color, his eyes lifeless. You can see it in the video. Lining up alongside Japan's Yasushi Kuroiwa, Jansen said he could feel his legs shaking at the starting line. He jumped early at the first gun and had to reorient himself. On the second gun, he got off to a decent start and made it through the first one hundred. But on the first turn, he took four strides and fell. You can slow down the footage to analyze where he lost his footing, but it almost doesn't matter. If Jansen didn't fall then, you get the sense he would have fallen eventually.

In any other context, the race for Jansen would have been devastating. He had spent the four years since Sarajevo building toward another Olympics, and when he got there, he didn't even manage to go the length of the rink without hurtling into the padded walls around the ice. In a perverse sense this time, he was spared seeing it that way, because the race was stripped of all significance.

"It was all so fast. Granted, the day was the longest day of my life, but then the race happened and ten seconds in, I was down," he says now. "You don't know what to do. I had to do press conferences and talk to people. I just wanted to go to my room and mourn my sister, but I had to talk about this race that lacked importance at the time."

Had this been the only event he had to compete in during those Olympics, perhaps Jansen's narrative would have been different. It was one race, and it happened to fall on the same day of his sister's death. But it wasn't Jansen's only race in Calgary. In a surge of emotion following the 500 meters, he declared he would win his next race, the 1,000 meters, for Jane. But Jansen didn't win this one, either. In fact, again he couldn't even remain upright. For two laps of a two-and-a-half-lap race, he was in the lead, and then his legs gave out and he found himself back on the ice. How to explain one of the best skaters in the world, just a week removed from winning a world championship, falling in consecutive races? The answer might be that in both mind and spirit, Jansen was never really there.

"That wasn't Dan Jansen skating," Peter Mueller, Jansen's longtime coach, said at the time. "That was his body, but it wasn't him. That man was in shock. I don't think he knew it himself."

* * *

WITH THE CONCLUSION of the Calgary Games, Jansen had been to two Olympics, skated in four races, and claimed zero medals. This is not unlike the fate of most Olympians, so that alone wasn't cause for panic. But Jansen wasn't just any Olympian. He was the best American male skater since Eric Heiden, a star of the 1980 Olympics who won five gold medals at Lake Placid. Jansen, too, was a once-a-decade talent, and he had the world records (he would end up setting eight in his career) and titles in non-Olympic events to prove it. After falling that second time in Calgary, there was reason for those around him to fear his failures would start to weigh on his psyche.

In the aftermath of his second Olympics, Jansen liked to joke that his full name might as well have been Dan Jansen "The Guy Who Fell on the Day His Sister Died," because every story written about him looked and sounded alike. I'm in the media. I get it. Once we find a storyline we like, we're content to ride it as long as we can. As the sportswriting legend Dan Jenkins said in *Golf Digest*, "The best writers are those who know how to recognize that defining moment and hammer it in their stories." For the Olympic media, "Dan Jansen fell twice" was just a nail waiting to be flattened.

The problem is those angles, while compelling to writers, risk making someone like Jansen resentful of how he's portrayed. Much like Bill Buckner or Greg Norman, Jansen was too easily defined by his mistakes, and there was growing concern it was chipping away at his confidence. In 1991, with the 1992 Winter Olympics in Albertville, France, approaching, Jansen's agent, Bennett Raffer, became leery of the recurring questions about Dan's ordeal in 1988 and suggested the skater work with Dr. Jim Loehr, the noted sports psychologist who oversees the Human Performance Institute in Orlando. This was about more than protecting an athlete's ego but rather disrupting the vicious cycle of thinking you're fated to lose.

"His agent called me and said, 'If we don't do something, Dan will go down as the greatest choker in sports history, or at least the greatest speed skater never to win an Olympic moment,'" Loehr recalls. "He really didn't think Dan could get over it on his own."

Loehr's work is helping people maximize their potential in fields such as sports and business. If you recall from chapter 1, he is a proponent of "framing" the events in our lives in as constructive a way as possible while also holding firm to the truth. Although the doctor had worked with a number of elite athletes, including tennis players and golfers he helped shepherd to major titles, Jansen admits he was initially skeptical of working with him. "I guess I never saw it in those terms, that I was freaking out and needed to talk to somebody," he says. Eventually, though, Jansen relented, and good thing—the connection with Loehr was likely the transformative moment of his career. Which is not to say that Jansen turned the corner right away, because there would still be more Olympic disappointments to come. To think anything would be easy for Jansen is to underestimate the extent of his journey.

ONCE THE SPECTACLE of the Olympics passes, you might think these athletes spend years obsessively counting down to the next games, like a prisoner scratching on the walls of his jail cell the days until his release. But Jansen says it's not like that, that the years in between are filled with ample distraction: speed skating World Cup meets and world championships, not to mention the endless training sessions. Jansen even knocked out some college credits while training with the US team in Calgary.

"Of course the Olympics are the ultimate goal, but you're taking it a year at a time and that year is what you're focused on. If all you're thinking about is the Olympics, you're finished," he says.

The mistake casual observers of these obscure sports make is thinking the Olympics are the only competitions that matter. But that's what made Jansen's record so confounding. He had won forty-six World Cup races in his career. He lost very infrequently, but because those losses tended to come in the races broadcast around the world, he and his supporters felt unfulfilled. And as much as Jansen restrained himself from thinking about the Olympics nonstop in the quiet years in between, he became more fixated on his next opportunity as the Albertville Olympics in France drew nearer.

In the month before the 1992 Games, Jansen was primed. He skated the two best 500-meter races of his life, including a world record on January 25, weeks before the Olympics. Although only in the very early stages of his work with Dr. Loehr, he still had plenty reason to believe he'd come home with some color medal. How could he not? He was four years wiser, skating better than ever, and while he would never get over the tragedy of losing Jane, the suddenness of his sister's death was no longer a crippling, destructive force.

"In his mind he was going to win," Mike Jansen says. "To us '88 was a whole different story, but by then he's got world record after world record and now here's his chance. . . . And again it didn't happen."

What happened in Albertville? A lot of things, actually, but one mistake was Dan's focusing on the outcome over the process. I've referenced this before. It's an important point when discussing how we approach winning and losing. The reason sports psychologists stress process goals over outcome goals is because the former allow you to focus on the things you can control as opposed to those you can't. If you recall my earlier example, a process goal would be a tennis player focusing on his breathing patterns and his stroke rather than where the ball lands. For an actor, it would be preparing as best you can for an audition and not fixating on whether you'll get the part. Meanwhile, an outcome goal would be Greg Norman's entertaining thoughts of winning a green jacket before he teed off in final round of the Masters. With outcome goals, there is no room for error.

"Focusing on the outcomes you want to get out of every day is important, but outcomes can be intimidating and at their worst, downright discouraging," writes Chris Bailey, a writer and speaker whose research on productivity culminated in a best-selling book, *The Productivity Project*. "Process goals will get you thinking about what you actually have to do to achieve your outcomes, and I think make you a lot more successful in achieving [them]."

Jansen's mistake in the Olympics wasn't that he abandoned his process of preparing exhaustively for competition, because he was always willing to put in the requisite work. But in the Olympics, he admits now, he couldn't help but think about the result.

"That was one difference in the Olympics versus non-Olympics—is that maybe I thought about how when the race is over, I'll be Olympic champion," he says. "I would never, ever think that in the world championships. There's definitely a lesson to be learned in there for anybody. Focusing too much on the reward and not on how to get there can be detrimental."

The failures of Albertville, in which he finished fourth in the 500- and twenty-sixth in the 1,000-meter races were less dramatic than Calgary in the sense that there were no falls and no family tragedy to shake him. So why did he lose? Was it really just the wrong mindset? Some in the media speculated he first needed to feel what it was like to end an Olympic race on his feet. Others pointed to the rain-softened ice, which was better suited for a skater with a shorter, choppier stride than Jansen's. Lastly, there's this:

the Olympics are hard, almost unreasonably so—too much time and energy funneled into races that last mere seconds, too much pressure heaped on the people who are supposed to perform, too much of an opportunity for those who aren't burdened in the same way to take advantage.

"You look at every single Olympics I've been involved with, either competing or working at it, there's always somebody who is middle of the pack who wins a medal, and sometimes wins gold," Jansen says. "Because you've got so much pressure on you as the favorite going in and it just becomes where you want to do it for everybody. It's a tough thing to deal with."

In 1988, Jansen felt guilty for being in Calgary while his sister was dying. Now he felt guilty for letting everyone around him down in not winning—his coaches, his agent, his family. After his 500-meter race, he had breakfast with his father, and Jansen wasn't sure what to expect, the memories of "There's more to life than skating around in a circle" still rattling around in his head. This time, though, Harry Jansen played it straight. He told Dan he was proud of him. He told him he knew he was better than the three skaters who beat him, but that for some reason it just didn't happen. And then Harry looked at Dan soberly and said, "You're my hero."

In speeches, Jansen tells that story and says he felt as though he could walk on air. "For some reason it just made everything OK," Jansen recalls. "It was truly a moment in my life I'll never forget."

Implicit in his father's message was that he didn't care

whether Dan had a medal because from his perspective, his son had already succeeded—not in winning, but in putting everything he could into his skating, and that's all a father could ask. Harry Jansen wasn't up to speed on his sports psychology lingo, but he was essentially telling his son that he admired how much Dan honored the process, even those times when he peeked ahead at the result.

The Jansens rolled out of France without a medal but at least with their dignity intact. Dan said all the right things, congratulated the winners, spoke of how much he was content to just enjoy the Olympic experience. More so than in winning, he says, it was in losing with humility and grace where he drew on the lessons from his family.

"Now having said that, did I have my moments?" he says. "Yeah, I had my moments. But the moments for me didn't last longer than the time it took to leave the arena that night. I made sure I went over to the guy who won and shook his hand and gave him a hug. Those are the things that are important to me, that I look back on with pride."

Had Jansen been forced to wait a traditional Olympic cycle for another chance at a medal, his story might have ended here. But it turns out the next Winter Olympics would be in 1994, just *two* years away, in Lillehammer, Norway.* It was a fortuitous bit of fate for a player contemplating the limited shelf life of a career, and Jansen was happy to take advantage. He was excited to get back on the

---

* The scheduling quirk was due to the International Olympic Committee's decision to no longer stage the Winter and Summer Games in the same year, as had been the case through 1992. The two events are now staggered every two years.

ice, but he knew that was not the only place he needed work. Jansen was prepared to give Dr. Loehr's counsel more attention than he had given it to that point. The two men decided that before they moved forward, they needed to spend some time looking back.

LOEHR WASN'T WORKING with Jansen when the skater's sister died and he fell twice in the span of four days in 1988. But Loehr had heard the stories, and now he had seen the tape. Look closer at that footage, Loehr says. The 500 meters fall was one thing—Jansen was on the ice that day, but his mind was elsewhere. But the 1,000 meters almost defied logic. Jansen was leading most of the way and on a world-record pace. He was on a straightaway with no one near him. The more Loehr watched the tape, the more he recognized that at that moment Jansen's subconscious took over and literally took his legs out from under him. In a strange way, Loehr says, Jansen wouldn't let himself win a gold medal, and the skater was still feeling the reverberations years later. To consider the depth of the two men's work together is to understand why their work prior to Albert-ville wasn't enough. Jansen still hadn't fully wrapped his brain around his past.

"He clearly needed to redefine and get back in control of his story," Loehr says.

Loehr's teachings are built around something called "cognitive restructuring," in which you essentially train your mind to think about an event differently than before.

This isn't about constructing a layer of fiction; truth is still paramount. If you struck out three times in a game, you're not going to start saying you went three-for-three with four RBIs. But there is a way to reshape the narrative to find a more palatable way of digesting what happened.

"Context and mindset are pretty much everything," Loehr explains. "The brain is always looking around trying to make sense of the experience, and we have this neuro-processing system that is very pliable and plastic. More important than what happens to you is the story and mindset you create around what happens."

As Loehr says, everything you confront is subject to an interpretation that *you* control. If you tell yourself you're a victim, you'll always be a victim. If you're convinced you're destined for a lifetime of Olympic disappointment, then you're probably not going to win an Olympic medal. Then again, if you begin to realize that your failings weren't actually failings in the first place, you can finally liberate yourself from a cloud of negativity.

An essential step in Loehr and Jansen's work together was Dan's coming to terms with the events around Jane's death. There had been hundreds of races, including world championships and Olympics in the years since. But on some fundamental level, Dan was still punishing himself, first for not being there when his sister passed, then in failing to win the 1,000-meter race that he dedicated to her days later. Yet in working with Loehr, a new narrative emerged that Dan began to recognize as true. With Jansen's blessing, Loehr shared what he told the skater:

I think it was because you cared so much about your sister that you fell in the 1,000 meters. You had the goal right in front of you and you were leading, and all you had to do was stand on your feet. [Falling] never happens to Dan Jansen. But from my perspective it happened because you wanted to give her the supreme gift you could give. You would deny yourself a gold medal so that she understood how much she meant to you. You could have gotten yourself a gold medal and crossed that line but you failed to do it. It was an act of courage more than it was a failure.

This breakthrough with Loehr proved to be the missing piece to Jansen's bouncing back from his defeats. It was an opportunity for the skater to reframe the traumatic episode that to that point had defined his career. Not only did it free him of the incredible guilt he felt for being at the Olympics when his sister died, but it opened him up to the type of "posttraumatic growth" that Loehr says has gained traction among psychologists. The opposite of posttraumatic stress disorder, in which a significant difficult experience has a continually debilitating impact on our lives, posttraumatic growth uses these events as a type of springboard for greater achievement and resilience.

"People actually get to a better place, a stronger place, and a higher level of excellence because they're able to weather the very difficult, gut-wrenching process of not succeeding, or in their eyes, failing," Loehr says.

To complete his transformation, Jansen had to do more than process his experience in 1988 differently. He and

Loehr also had to rethink how they were going to approach Jansen's two specialty races. His strength had always been the 500. It's a sprint, and Jansen is built like a sprinter, with big, powerful thighs that allow him to explode off the starting line and carry pretty much the same momentum through the half-minute race. The 1,000 was different because the longer distance worked against his body type. The bigger your muscles, the greater the buildup of lactic acid in them, the more you contend with fatigue in the race's later stages. It's why Jansen's MO in those races was always to jump out to a big lead and hold on as best he could. Sometimes it worked. Very often he faded.

In the two years between Albertville and Lillehammer, Jansen heard suggestions that he should give up on the 1,000 and just focus on the 500. The two races are distinct enough that his problem could have been spreading himself too thin. Why not just play to your strengths?

"It was more from other coaches, or people hanging around the rink, but it definitely came up," Jansen says. "[My coaches and I] never really considered it."

Still, the truth was that the 1,000 *was* the weaker event for Jansen. It's a race he came to dread, which is not uncommon: the more challenging you find an endeavor, the less likely you are to warm to it—which in turn further decreases your chances of success. This is a fixed mindset trait even the most resilient among us contend with, and Loehr and Jansen needed to find a way to disrupt the cycle. Here Loehr had an idea. Much as the psychologist Carol Dweck elicited better results from students by teaching them to enjoy challenge, Loehr's strategy was to convince Jansen to love the distance. He had taken a similar tack with a tennis player client who hated tiebreakers, and Loehr forced him to alter his thinking until he actually felt the opposite. With Jansen, Loehr went so far as to force him to write down each day on his training log, "I love the 1,000."

Jansen initially resisted. He said, "I can't do that because I don't."

Loehr countered that he would eventually. "I said, 'You're going to change your mind deliberately, and you're going to come to adore the 1,000, and as that happens, your body is going to start adapting in ways that build belief.'"

Eventually Jansen complied, writing the affirmation down on his log, and in a drawer in the bathroom, and on the mirror in his bedroom. Jansen was always faithful to the rituals of training, and Loehr had at least convinced him this was part of the deal.

"I first thought it was crazy," Dan says. "I thought, 'I'll do it, but why is this going to get me to actually like the race?' But what I learned is there is a strange power in actually writing. Handwriting, not typing. When you do it, it starts to become ritual, and then you start to believe it."

About a month before the Lillehammer Games, Jansen called Loehr.

"You know it's amazing," Jansen said, "but I think I love the 1,000 more than the 500."

*   *   *

IN A CRUEL bit of timing, Jansen's 500-meter race in the Lillehammer Games was on the six-year anniversary of his sister Jane's death. Even crueler is that after three Olympics and all this work on his body and mind, he lost again. He didn't fall, but he did slip toward the end, enough to have to reach down for the ice, lose valuable momentum, and tumble down the standings. He finished eighth.

Dan was in shock. His coach was in shock. In the stands, cameras showed Dan's then wife Robin (he has since remarried) rise from her seat and rush out of view so she couldn't be caught sobbing.

"It's almost impossible to chronicle the truckload of emotions that was going through my mind," Jansen wrote in *Full Circle*. "The first thing I did after the race was just kind of laugh to myself. It was the same kind of laugh that Sisyphus, the guy who kept pushing the rock up the hill only to watch it roll down again, must've laughed. The whole thing was just too ridiculous."

So it came down to the 1,000, Jansen's last race in any Olympics and his last chance to win a medal, and however disappointing the previous race had been, this is where his work with Loehr was realized: Whatever would happen, Dan was fine with it. Of course he wanted to win, and of course he'd be upset if he didn't. But this would be his final Olympics regardless, and he'd have a rich life ahead whether there was a medal in his possession or not. When it came to the concepts of counterfactual thinking and thinking about alternative scenarios, Dan could contemplate either outcome and know he'd be OK. When he addressed his family before his last race, he told them not to worry.

"He said, 'This is my last race, and whatever happens, just go out and have fun watching me, because that's what I plan to do,'" Mike Jansen recalls. "His sense was if he didn't get a medal, he'd still be happy [and we should be, too]."

When it came down to focusing on the process instead of the reward, Jansen realized the two had converged: The process *was* the reward. Running to the rink with his brothers with their skates in their hands, the painstaking effort to shave a fraction of a second off a split time, the ridiculous mantras he wrote on the top of his training logs— *these* were the spoils of his career as a skater. A medal could provide outside validation, but it couldn't replace the satisfaction he had already derived from striving to get there.

I realize this concept might have limits. No one interviews for a job out of the joy of interviewing. No one runs for political office because they want to hand out flyers on a street corner and make seven speeches a day. Sometimes the reward really is the point. But if you subscribe to the belief that all experience can be enriching, then you stand to benefit regardless of the outcome. That was the epiphany Dan Jansen had on the eve of his final Olympic race.

"If he hadn't succeeded, Dan would have been fine," Loehr says. "If he thought this was the end of the world, he would have not done well, but he created a mindset where this was a chance to show the world what a gift speed skating had been for him. He loved it, and he hoped to be able to leave it with an Olympic medal. But if he didn't, it still had been a great gift. It kind of transformed into a sense of realization and peace. Once the gun went off, it sort of clicked: 'You're not a failure if you lose.'"

At the beginning of this chapter, I said the misconception is that Dan Jansen's life changed when he won a gold medal. This is the part about his story people get wrong. Because all signs prior to his 1,000-meter race in Lillehammer were that he would have flourished even in defeat, and what a lesson that would have been for the rest of us. But that's not what happened. In the 1,000 that day, Dan skated the race of his life, set a world record, and later pulled his baby daughter out of the stands for a victory lap. Of course her name is Jane. For many Olympics, the filmmaker Bud Greenspan profiled a handful of compelling Olympic stories, and in 1994, Jansen was one of them. I dare you to watch the moment when Jansen looks up at his time after crossing the finishing line and not well with tears. Or maybe that's just me.

I PUT THE question to Jansen: What would your life be like if you hadn't won? It's impossible to answer, of course. But he's clearly thought about it.

"It's not a comfortable thought," he says. "I wouldn't have been asked to speak as much as I speak. I wouldn't be invited to things as a celebrity. But at the same time, I wouldn't be any different. I'd be the same person. I worked just as hard. I was still as good as I was, which was the best in the world. But if it didn't happen in that 1:12 . . ."

His voice trails off. He is right: if it didn't happen in that 1:12, no one would pay $15,000 for the guy who fell flat at four Olympics to come speak at their sales meeting. You can tell Jansen is embarrassed by this proposition. There are men he lived and trained with, including his brother Mike, whose skating careers amounted to little more than a collection of dusty newspaper clips. And then there's an even more difficult thought.

"The other elephant in the room, and Dan has said it before, is that a lot of his success is because of his sister," Jansen's wife, Karen Palacios-Jansen, says. "Maybe his story wouldn't be so powerful if someone didn't lose their life. Maybe that's why he's embarrassed. But at the same time, that's what happened. That's what his story is. His family is OK with it. He's done a lot of good with this tragedy. He's helped a lot of people."

Jansen is in his early fifties now. He lives in Charlotte, North Carolina, where he moved to be closer to his two daughters after his divorce from his first wife. In addition to his speaking engagements, he sells medical equipment and real estate, has dabbled in sports commentary, and oversees the Dan Jansen Foundation, which raises money for a number of charities, most notably fighting leukemia. His greatest contribution, though, is as a model of persistence. He is reminded of this all the time, by people who've reached out in person or by mail about the passing of a loved one or a loss in this race or that. "At times I feel like a psychologist," Jansen says. He's had no formal training, but that's one thing Dan knows his father got wrong. You'd be amazed how much you can learn about life just skating around in a circle.

7

"Good Things Come Out of Chaos": A Soccer Player's Powerful Rebirth

The wound is the place where the Light enters you.
—RUMI

DAN JANSEN'S STORY at least followed a familiar trajectory. The hard parts came first. He endured personal and professional losses, struggled to learn from them, and eventually went on to parlay those experiences into a climactic crowning achievement. It was a conventional three-act narrative. All you needed was a string section for the soundtrack.

Suppose, though, that the order was reversed. What if the crowning achievement comes first and then all the heartache and losing follows? In some ways that's the most daunting chronology of all.

A quick story: When I was a freshman in college, I collapsed my lung in a tackle football game with my friends over Thanksgiving. I was in the hospital for two weeks and now have a massive scar across my back that looks like the remnants of a shark bite. Most of the rest of the ordeal is a distant memory, but what I distinctly remember is lying in the hospital right after it happened and my brother shaking his head. "This ends, like, the world's longest winning streak," he said. Josh wasn't talking about sports, and he certainly wasn't referencing some dizzying string of successes with school or girls or whatever. But it was his impression that I had cruised through my first eighteen years, and he wasn't entirely wrong. I was a fairly happy kid growing up. I had close friends, assimilated well enough in school and on various teams, and while my athletic career was littered with disappointments, it was pretty manageable stuff when compared to a chest tube jammed into my side and a stay in the ICU. As Josh saw it, this was the first time I had truly been knocked on my ass. And in the absence of any precedent, he had reason to wonder if I even knew how to get back up.

SARA WHALEN HESS's story is far more dramatic than mine. But hers, too, is about falling from a lofty perch and at first not knowing how to handle it. It's about how adversity forces you to summon a part of yourself that you might not have known existed—a painful journey that, navigated properly, can be empowering.

Like me, Hess didn't come across many setbacks as a kid, and she admits she wasn't well equipped to handle those that she did. Now a psychologist and a mother of three, she recognizes the distinction between growth mindsets and fixed mindsets as the difference between kids who throw themselves into situations without fear of consequences and those who abstain for fear of failing. Looking back at her childhood, Sara says she was more like my oldest, Charlie, holding just a little back because she didn't want to screw up.

"I was more 'I'm just not going to try that hard because I don't want to be embarrassed if I don't succeed,'" she says. "That was sort of my MO."

When Hess went to the University of Connecticut to play soccer, she was lured out of that shell. Although a promising athlete growing up on Long Island, she was far from a superstar, owing in part to an attitude that prevented her from giving everything she had. She headed to UConn without assurances of a scholarship, and it wasn't until pushed by the Huskies' gruff Greek-born coach, Lenny Tsantiris, that she began to shed her apprehension.

It's always remarkable to me how the leadership qualities that are laid out in seminars and shelves' worth of self-help books arise in some people instinctively. Tsantiris wasn't a conventional motivator. He has a thick accent and lacks a great grasp of social nuance, which is part of what makes him more direct than many girls who come under his watch are accustomed to. But Hess soon recognized that beneath Tsantiris's blunt exterior was someone who believed in her.

"I think he and his staff felt I could do a lot more, and I figured if they felt that way, it was probably true," she says. "Up to that point I'm not sure I had that confidence in myself. But with Lenny it was a lot of 'Cut the shit and let's go.' Instead of, you know, 'Everything is going to be OK. Everything's fine,' it was 'We're going to watch two hours of video, and we're going to fix this problem.' And I loved that because it was clear cut and understood."

Under Tsantiris, Hess flourished. She played well enough her freshman season to be awarded a full scholarship and was even invited that year to train with the US Women's National Team. It was only a short stay, but the experience was still instructive, and Hess left hopeful she would be given another crack before long. Then as a senior, Hess enjoyed the defining moment of her collegiate career when she led the Huskies to the NCAA Final Four. Facing heavily favored Notre Dame in the semis, Hess scored both of her team's goals in a 2–1 win. It was a massive upset, to the extent that the Huskies' loss in the national championship game that followed seemed irrelevant. Like eighteen-year-old Dan Jansen finishing fourth at Sarajevo, the team and its star forward had already exceeded expectations.

"That was all I ever wanted in the world," she says. "I didn't care what happened in the final because I felt like I met my max."

Actually, she hadn't. The day after the NCAA finals, Hess was on a plane to Brazil to rejoin the National Team, which took on an added importance with the Women's World Cup to be played in the United States the following year. Three years after walking on at UConn, she was on the precipice of playing for the host country in the most important tournament in the world. The National Team—which featured legends of women's soccer such as Mia Hamm, Julie Foudy, and Michelle Akers—was an intensely focused, tight-knit group. At times, Hess felt like she was out of her depth, but she was determined to fit in.

"I was used to being about me, me, me, but now you have these amazing people who not only work so hard but work so hard for you," she says. "I decided I wanted to help any way I can for this team. I'm going to work my ass off for these guys, which is the totally mature view."

Although Hess was coming off three consecutive first-team All-American seasons at UConn, the talent pool on the National Team was so deep that a spot on the team was far from a certainty. The group was always fluid, with players shuttling in and out often. She had played forward her senior season in college, but US coach Tony DiCicco moved Hess to back, where as one of the team's speediest players, she could quickly jump into the attack. When the US played Japan about a month before the World Cup, DiCicco was still deciding between Hess and another player for the final roster, and Hess responded with a resounding performance, at one point racing fifty yards with the ball to score.

"That did it for me. She knew she had to perform in that game, and she did," DiCicco tells me. "That was a great statement that she could raise her game when it mattered."

So she was on the team, but Hess had to accept that her role had limits. With so many established players, many of whom were part of the gold medal–winning US team in the 1996 Olympics, it was difficult for Hess to identify someone she should be replacing in the lineup. At times she struggled with the same confidence issues she first showed up with at UConn. But at least DiCicco believed in her enough to use her as a reserve. And at least she was there at all.

"It was very hard because at any point you can go from starting to subbing, from subbing to bubble, and from bubble to 'See you later.' You're always on your game," she says. "So for me it was a great feeling knowing I had a role and I was an important part of the team."

Hess recently turned forty. She is pretty, with big, expressive eyes and the same athletic figure she had two decades ago. When we meet one day for coffee, she is often animated in telling her story, never more so than when describing her experience in the World Cup. It's an important part of her journey, particularly when contrasted with the painful ordeal that would follow. To appreciate the depths of someone's pain, it helps to identify the heights from which they have fallen.

It's not a stretch to say that the US team that year was the most important women's sports team in history. The Women's World Cup came around at a time when women's sports, especially soccer, were beginning to boom in this country, and the end was a classic, with ninety thousand people at the Rose Bowl and forty million viewers at home—many of whom were tuning into a women's sport for the first time.

The Americans had rolled through the early part of the tournament—a packed house against Denmark at Giants Stadium, another one against Nigeria at Soldier Field, and so on—and Hess played well coming off the bench. Then came the final against China in Pasadena, the stands jammed, flags waving, the score stuck at 0–0. When DiCicco tapped her to replace the injured Michelle Akers in the second half, Hess overcame early nerves and played well through the end of regulation and overtime. But there were still no goals, which led to the climactic series of penalty kicks. Hess was scheduled to be the ninth shooter, and she was mortified at the thought that the entire thing could come down to her.

"The whole time, we were like 'God, don't let it get to me. Please God, don't let it get to me. Please God, let this game end before it gets to me,'" she says. "And thankfully it did."

There would be no ninth round. When US goalie Briana Scurry stopped the fourth Chinese shooter, it opened the door for Brandi Chastain's indelible Cup-clinching moment: burying her shot into the right corner of the goal to win the game, ripping off her shirt, and dropping to her knees in just a sports bra. The Rose Bowl exploded. Her teammates raced toward her. The first one there was Sara Hess, the ensuing celebration captured by a swarm of cameras. The scene was the next week's cover of *Time* magazine, Hess featured most prominently of all.

THE SUMMER WAS a whirlwind. The women appeared on *Letterman*. There were commercial deals and more celebrity appearances. Nike featured Hess in a two-page ad that ran in magazines like *Vogue* and *Elle*, not to mention a giant billboard in front of Chelsea Piers in Manhattan.

For Hess, this should have been just the beginning. She was among the youngest players on the team, just a year removed from college, and when the US returned to international competition later that summer, DiCicco elevated her to a starting role. With the 2000 Olympics in Sydney, Australia, approaching, both player and coach envisioned her being central to the Americans' chances.

"She was a young player just starting to make her mark," DiCicco says. "I saw her as a big part of the National Team's future."

DiCicco was a lot like Tsantiris for Hess in that he had to cut through the player's insecurities to build her up. It wasn't a stretch because the talent was real. But it was apparent that Hess depended on reassurance more than her teammates.

"When she was younger and she had a bad day it stuck with her," Hess's mother, Linda Whalen, says. "I felt like Tony was the one who gave her the confidence."

Where things started to go awry is when DiCicco stepped down as coach of the National Team to spend more time with his family. At the outset, the Americans seemed to have landed the right replacement in April Heinrichs, herself a former US World Cup player and collegiate soccer star who was now looking to build on the foundation DiCicco had laid.

The problem was that Hess and Heinrichs clashed right from the start. It's pointless to try to assess blame. Hess will be the first to admit she was temperamental, and Heinrichs thought it important to make a mark distinct from DiCicco's. Because of that, though, Hess grew resentful of how little regard Heinrichs and her staff had for the progress the player had already made. It was as if Hess had spent all this time building up capital only to discover her currency was worthless. She remembers an early practice under Heinrichs and her staff, when a new assistant coach lined the team up for a drill and asked everyone for their names. Normally this wouldn't have been a big deal, but remember, many of them had been plastered across magazine covers and billboards in recent months.

"And I was like, 'Are you serious? Did you watch the World Cup?'" Hess recalls. "For some reason it crushed me on a whole new level, and I was like, 'I can't do this again. I can't rebuild.' So I started with zero confidence. And then I began to play poorly."

For all her growth, Hess was still the girl reluctant to mess up for fear of being embarrassed. With Tsantiris and DiCicco, there was always an undercurrent of support, every harsh sentence framed in the context of their belief in her. But Heinrichs came at it from a different perspective. These girls had just won the World Cup and were hailed at every turn. How much more positive reinforcement did they need?

As the US National Team started making its push for the Sydney Olympics and new players were brought into the mix, Hess's playing time plummeted and with it her self-esteem. The more Heinrichs pushed her, the more Hess withdrew, to the point that she was unable to hear anything other than criticism.

"Tony kind of understood the level beneath the attitude," Hess recalls. "I just needed a little encouragement. But April was always pointing out the things that were wrong, without the 'Come on, you can do better.' I felt like I was only taking in negative feedback."

It was with this as a backdrop that Hess boarded a plane for Sydney and her first Olympics. The last part of that sentence sounds so romantic. The Olympics! The opening ceremonies! Every young athlete dreams of such an opportunity, Hess included. Which may explain why reality was such a disappointment.

SARA HESS AND I live in the same town. We have friends in common and occasionally end up at the same events with our kids. The first time I met her husband, Jon, I was actually playing in *another* friendly football game in which I got hurt and wound up in the hospital. I wish I was making this up. There was a decent amount of blood, and Jon gave me his extra T-shirt to sop it up, and I remember as I walked to my car on the way to the emergency room, I called out, "But what about your shirt?"

"I don't want that shirt back," he said.

What I knew about the Hesses was that Jon had been a lacrosse star at Princeton and Sara had played soccer at some high level. But that was pretty much it. I thought of them as just another accomplished couple with a rich history to share with their friends. Our suburban town is full of them. Only later did I learn Sara was as big a deal in soccer as she was. Once I knew more of the details of her story, I asked her what she says to people when they ask about her experience in the Olympics.

"I lie," she says. "I tell them it was amazing."

Hess hated the Olympics. She walked in the opening ceremonies, and that was fun, but it was also the most action she saw while there. The US played five games in Australia, including the gold medal match they lost in overtime to Norway, and Hess never played a minute in any of them. You might say, so what? Plenty of athletes make it to the Olympics as benchwarmers and are still able to savor the experience. But this is why the order of things is so important. Hess was just a year removed from the incredible high of the World Cup, playing in front of massive crowds. She was a reserve but a valuable reserve, and in her mind, her role was supposed to only increase over time. It goes back to that concept of counterfactual thinking—focusing more on what could have been as opposed to what actually happened. To Hess, the Olympics should have followed the track she was on under DiCicco. She should have been starting, or at least playing. The Americans should have been playing in front of packed stadiums instead of less than ten thousand people three hours outside Sydney. They should have won gold.

"Not one part of it was amazing," she says. "I cried most of my time in the Olympics in Australia. I remember crying so much I literally couldn't get out of bed."

Overcome by depression, Hess was also eating less, a problem that was brought to the fore upon returning to the

United States. The Americans had a team psychologist to whom she had divulged her feelings of desolation as well as her irregular eating habits. Hess thought their sessions were confidential, but when she sat down to meet with the coaching staff, she says, she heard many of the details of those conversations echoed back to her.

"April brought it up to me in a meeting, and I thought that was horrible," Hess says. "She said, 'You're not eating. You know what happens when you don't eat. That's why you're not strong.' And I was like, 'Oh my God, I'm out.' That was going to be hard to play for her after that. I didn't want to be there anymore."

(I reached out to Heinrichs to ask about her time coaching Hess, and she said that she didn't recall this episode. She added: "I'm sorry to hear that. There are players who rise to the National Team in the face of adversity like depression, and I have to commend Sara if that was one of the things going on in her life at the time.")

Players don't just quit the National Team. The opportunities are too few, the road to get there too tough, the privilege too great. But Hess didn't care about all that. She was miserable. The previous winter, she and nineteen other players from the World Cup–winning US squad became founding members of a new professional league, the Women's United Soccer Association (WUSA), with Hess signed up to play for the league's New York Power. So it wasn't as if she would be leaving soccer altogether. But the National Team was a weight she felt needed to be lifted, so one day Hess walked into Heinrichs's office to tell her she wouldn't be reporting to the next training camp. According to Hess, Heinrichs replied that if she wasn't at training camp, she might as well not come back. Hess said that was precisely her goal.

When Hess returned to her room to report to roommate Lorrie Fair that she had quit, the prevailing emotion was relief.

"Good for you," Fair said.

"Oh my God," Hess replied, surprised by her emotions. "I feel so much better."

How you deal with losing depends on how you frame it. As Dr. Jim Loehr says, it's the narrative we wrap around an event that ultimately dictates how we feel about it. In Hess's case, the end of her National Team career could have been devastating had she dwelled on everything she was giving up. Her mother, for instance, originally thought she was making a big mistake. "Who quits the National Team?" Linda Whalen asked. But Sara chose to focus on what she'd be gaining in return. She could move back to New York to focus on playing pro soccer. She could be freed from the strain of playing for a coach who didn't value her. And since by then she was serious with Jon, she could now be something more than a voice at the other end of a cell phone.

It was a loss, sure, but she was prepared to weather it. Compared to the next part, in fact, it was a breeze.

REMEMBER HOW HESS described the fleeting status players were afforded on the National Team—from starting to subbing, all the way down to "See you later"? It turns out Hess traveled an even darker path, from starting on the National Team, to off the team, to playing soccer elsewhere, to getting hurt so badly you start questioning whether you even want to live. It was all there, Hess passing through each checkpoint in a procession that alternately felt too fast or never ending.

It had started out innocuously enough. When Hess moved to Manhattan to begin her career with the fledgling New York Power, she was beginning to emerge from the funk of the previous year. She was making decent money from her contract as a WUSA founding member as well as from endorsements; she was relishing living in the city; and most surprisingly, she was again having fun playing soccer.

"It was a really positive experience," Jon Hess, Sara's then boyfriend and now husband, says. "The soccer was great, the friends were great, the laughs were great. She had money in her pocket. It was just one of those times when everything was going right."

As quickly as the joy of the game had been sucked out of Sara, that's how quickly it was restored, owing mostly to the fact that she had divorced herself from a difficult situation and was back playing well. Although she and Jon had been dating since shortly after the 1999 World Cup, he never had much of a chance to really watch her play. His reaction once he saw her dart up the field with a ball seemingly tethered to her feet was "Holy crap, she's really good."

In fact, Sara was so encouraged by her success with the Power, she quietly started contemplating a road back to the

National Team. The next World Cup was two years away, and she had eyes on being there. Whether Heinrichs would accept her back was a question Hess couldn't answer, and for reasons that soon became clear, she wouldn't need to. Because then came the WUSA All-Star Game in Florida in 2002. Playing defense, Hess took an aggressive angle on an opposing forward, Shannon MacMillan, who was bearing down on goal. The two collided awkwardly, and Hess ended up breaking her ribs and puncturing her lungs.

Later, Hess said she recognized this as "the beginning of my demise." There was no real medical correlation between this injury and the trouble she would later confront, but in retrospect, she says it signaled a change. Hess had never had any injuries save for the occasional tender hamstring, but this was serious enough to sideline her indefinitely. She couldn't even fly because her lungs were vulnerable to changes in air pressure. She was out for two months, and soon after she returned, she was in a game against Carolina and their forward Birgit Prinz, a star of the German National Team. Hess tried to make a head-on tackle on Prinz, another aggressive play since Prinz was a powerful specimen.

"She's bigger than you and I combined," Hess tells me, "and my leg just lost that battle."

For several years MTV had a show called *Scarred* that showcased various grisly injuries and told the stories behind them. Hess's injury, including the graphic footage from her confrontation with Prinz, was bad enough to be featured. She had torn her ACL and her meniscus and a handful of other ligaments in her right knee, and her season was over. Yet even then, Hess had eyes on playing soccer again. Knee injuries are ever present in women's soccer—women are roughly six times more likely to tear their ACLs than men are. The good news is recovery is commonplace, too, and Hess figured she'd do her stint in rehab and get back out there.

"My mentality was still, 'I'm in,'" she says. "'We'll just do this.'"

But something wasn't right. It was more than just the expected pain Hess felt from her injury and the subsequent surgery. She felt terrible everywhere. She would drag herself to physical therapy but always under this lethargic, feverish haze. It went on for weeks, and no one was quite sure why. Then one day Hess had her cousin Dr. Beth Shubin Stein, who was an orthopedic surgeon at New York's Hospital for Special Surgery, check out her knee, and that's when they discovered an alarming fluid oozing from it. Hess learned her knee was severely infected, and she needed an immediate surgery to wash it out. It was worrisome, but Hess remembers feeling mostly relieved that they found the root of the problem. She packed a bag for the hospital.

Once she was on the operating table, with her cousin in the room, doctors started by washing Hess's knee with an intravenous fluid. But once they added the antibiotic bacitracin to the compound, Hess said she began to feel as if she were on fire.

"She said her chest felt heavy and she couldn't breathe, and we knew right away it was an anaphylactic reaction," Shubin Stein says.

The surgery was now a scramble. Since it was clear Hess was allergic to the bacitracin, the medicine needed to be flushed out of her system. Meanwhile her blood pressure had dropped so alarmingly low doctors needed to intubate her to keep her airways open. Hess was awake but now paralyzed by the intubation, which doctors call feeling "locked in the box." For several harrowing minutes, doctors were forced to wait to see if Hess's system could regulate. Eventually, she passed out.

When Hess awoke, she still had a tube in her throat and couldn't move, and now she was being told by doctors how close she came to dying. If the intended effect was to make her feel better, it didn't work.

"I remember thinking, 'Why are you telling me this? Please don't tell me this,'" she recalls. "And I felt so sick, I still felt like I was dying."

As traumatic as the surgery had been, it didn't solve the problem it was intended to rectify. The infection was still there; Hess still felt awful, and now because she was in such a vulnerable state, she was told she needed time before doctors could go back in and fix what ailed her. Her condition deteriorated. In playing shape, she was a sinewy 135 pounds, but her illness had whittled her down to 100. She was so weak that once she did leave the hospital several weeks later, she was forced to move out of her apartment and back in with her parents on Long Island. Whatever antibiotics doctors put Hess on, she turned out to be allergic to those as well. This once strong, energetic athlete was now so sick her parents had to carry her down to the couch in the morning and carry her back up at night.

"I can't even begin to tell you how awful it was," her mother says. "It was painfully awful."

Sara remembers Jon's visits during this time as essentially her vomiting nonstop for thirty minutes. Even once she regained enough strength to return to her own apartment, her roommate says it was like splitting the rent with a ghost.

"In so many ways it was like a bad movie, like how is she living through this?" says Jen O'Sullivan Driscoll, a New York Power teammate who shared an apartment with Hess in Manhattan. "It wasn't just physical pain. She was in a deep depression. You'd come back to the apartment, and there'd be little life there. She was in a terrible place."

The ordeal was two-pronged. Hess felt chronically weak; her appetite vanished to the point that her family was trying to force-feed her protein shakes. But with all that came the slow realization that her soccer career, what she identified with most of all, was slipping from her grasp. Hess's life seemed to be passing her by, and at times she questioned whether she wanted it to continue.

"It's just, you can't feel that way indefinitely," she says. "Your body can only sustain so much pain. You know when you have the flu and it lasts like two or three days, you're like, 'I can't take it'? You can't live like that on a daily basis. There were moments of extreme vomiting with a one-hundred-and-five-degree fever, and it was like, 'Just fucking end it. I can't deal with this anymore.'"

*　*　*

A CONFOUNDING TYPE of losing is a loss of self. It doesn't matter how it's lost. Think back to the former baseball commissioner Fay Vincent falling out a fourth-story window, breaking his back, and then having to recalibrate a life that could no longer include football. Vincent blamed himself for his hubris. He called it "a failure of judgment." The loss he experienced was akin to Sara Hess contemplating an existence that felt centuries removed from the day she sprinted to midfield at the Rose Bowl. Both were forced to grieve a piece of themselves.

To understand this dynamic, consider what the psychologist Abraham Maslow famously coined our "hierarchy of needs." Maslow's landmark paper, written in 1943, theorized that human motivation can be broken into five layers of a pyramid. The pyramid looks like this:

At the bottom are the physiological elements essential to human survival like food and shelter, followed by nearly as pressing concerns over health and security. Beyond that, the needs become more nuanced, but they all play a role in a contented and meaningful existence. Love and belonging appeal to our tribal nature and our desire to be accepted. Esteem is our wanting to be respected, while self-actualization speaks to our need to fulfill our individual potential. As Maslow writes, "the appearance of one need usually rests on the prior satisfaction of another, more pre-potent need." In other words, you first need to be nourished, safe, and loved before you can worry about whether your colleagues at work think highly of you or whether you're doing enough to maximize your talents. (The hierarchy of needs also underscores the idea that rich people don't have fewer problems, they just have *different* problems.)

Regardless, Hess losing her soccer career cut into a number of needs: the need for belonging in that she had lost her community, the need for esteem in that she had lost the status of being a professional athlete, and the need for self-actualization in that she was deprived of a chance to do something she did quite well. Maslow's hierarchy proves all losing is relative, since anyone who's ever begged for a hot meal or a place to sleep might have a hard time feeling sorry for Hess. Similarly, a driving range pro charging fifty dollars a lesson would love to trade places with Greg Norman even as he was in the throes of blowing the Masters. But as Maslow said, "man is a perpetually wanting animal," so it's hard for us to simply be satisfied with what we have.

The good news for Hess is that over the ensuing months she began to emerge from the depths of her worst physical pain. It wasn't easy, or quick, and she still deals with a version of it more than a dozen years after her violent collision with Prinz. The other day I texted her a question following up on our interviews, and she asked if she could call me in ten minutes. Right then she was busy receiving another injection in her knee.

Slowly Hess began to piece back together a life, and this process was no less impressive than Dan Jansen's overcoming years of Olympic struggle to win gold in the 1,000 meters. An essential step was to deal with the most pressing concerns around her knee. If she wasn't worried about the joint in the context of a soccer career, she still had something causing an adverse reaction, and she still needed to find a way to function as an independent adult. She and Jon were headed down a road that they hoped would lead to marriage and kids, neither of which seemed plausible in her current condition. So Sara was slated for two surgeries— the first in which doctors would remove the hardware in her leg, which was from the original surgery and may have led to the infection, and a second in which doctors would try again to graft in a ligament from a cadaver. One problem with accepting an outside ligament in her body, though, was the risk of traces of bacitracin, so a last-minute plan was devised in which doctors would pull a part of the patella tendon out of her left knee and put it in the right knee. It eliminated the unknown, but it also meant Hess was now charged with rehabbing two knees at once.

OK, fine, Sara thought. *Whatever.* By this point she had been poked and prodded and wrapped in so many different knee braces, she was practically oblivious to the constant discomfort. Harder to fathom is how after all this time she had transformed into a completely different person. Soccer was over. None of her former teammates from the National Team even bothered to check on her, leading to feelings of resentment. And when she looked in the mirror, she hardly recognized who she saw.

"Especially early on there was a real feeling of loss, especially as her friends were continuing to play," Jon Hess says. "It's more than just playing soccer. These were her colleagues, and you lose that sense of purpose. When she'd look at a picture of herself from when she was playing soccer, she'd see this jacked-up athlete. Now she'd see herself and there was this person with no muscle tone."

An essential outlet for Hess came when she enrolled in a graduate psychology program at Fordham University. If at UConn school was just something to tide her over between soccer practices, she now needed her education to sustain her. For one thing, she had to occupy her time with something other than mindless rehab. But it was also the subject matter. As painful as the past few years had been, they gave Hess an understanding of emotional suffering she learned to see as an asset.

Hess recalls a guest speaker at Fordham. She doesn't remember his name, but she remembers his lecture resonating deeply, to the extent that after class, she hobbled up to him in her two knee braces and shared some of her history.

She referenced the end of her time on the National Team, the knee injury and subsequent surgeries, the feelings of alienation and bitterness. At this point, she was still raw, and skeptical that she could harness these swirling emotions enough to be an effective counselor.

"I said, 'After all this trauma, with me still feeling the repercussions, how's that going to translate into me being good at this job?'" Hess says. "He said, 'That's exactly the stuff that's going to make you amazing at this job.' He made me feel like it was only going to help me, which was totally a different mentality to take into my training."

It was a rare moment when Hess felt that she again had some ownership in her story, when she saw life as more than a collection of shitty things that had happened to her. The mindset permeated to other aspects of her life. Still in the throes of physical therapy, Hess felt as though she wasn't seeing any significant improvement in her knees, in part because the doctors and physical therapists were still cautious around the slightest pain. So one day Sara decided she needed a break. She wouldn't go back to rehab and would instead implement her own regimen on the West Side Highway. She would walk, and then if all went well, she would try to run, even if for just one minute.

"I was like, I can deal with pain for a minute," she says. "At this point I'm not thinking about soccer, but I am thinking about jogging with my kids one day, basic life stuff. So I went out every day for a minute. Then it became two minutes. And eventually it was five minutes."

The pain was so severe that Hess would occasionally run

in tears, but she persisted. Five minutes became ten minutes, then twenty. Then one day, Sara reported to friends and family that she was going to run that year's New York Marathon. By all objective measures, it was a terrible idea, perhaps the worst thing you can do with two bad knees. But there was no sense in trying to stop her.

"It was in her head," Linda Whalen says. "She said, 'I have to do this.'"

THESE TRANSFORMATIVE MOMENTS don't just announce themselves. As Dan Jansen said, it wasn't as if he fell at the Olympics, unlaced his skates, and asked himself how he was going to learn from it. "Life doesn't work that way," Jansen says.

What happens over time, though, is the landscape in front of you becomes the only one you know, and you're eventually forced to adapt. It's like Fay Vincent coming to terms with his broken back, or Greg Norman accepting a life without a Masters green jacket. What other choice did they have?

Sara Hess arrived at that same place. Her friend and former roommate Jen Driscoll recalls the marathon, when Hess ran toward a group of her friends at mile seventeen, and they reached over the barricades and essentially mobbed her, their excitement rivaled only by Sara's exhaustion. It was a deeply symbolic day, as marathons tend to be, and in Sara's case it was her way of saying she had not only regained the self she had lost but also emerged even stronger.

"We tackled her like we had just won the World Cup because we were all so proud of her," Driscoll says. "It was like she was making this dual statement that mentally and physically 'I'm going to reset myself.' I get chills even thinking about it now."

Hess's marathon, which she finished in four hours and nineteen minutes and which was featured in the *New York Times* (headline: AN ERSTWHILE SOCCER STAR FINDS A NEW LIFE IN RUNNING), was an example of her regaining control of her narrative. Another was in how she immersed herself in her new career. When Sara completed her master's degree in psychology from Fordham, Jon congratulated her, assuming the education part of her journey was complete. Sara swiftly replied that it wasn't. She would now go after her doctorate, and she already had a line on a worthy dissertation—athletic identity and the role it plays in one's self-worth. She would use a class of high school athletes as a focus group, but she might as well have written it straight from experience. Among her findings is that "athletes who place too strong an emphasis on athletics may experience psychological and physical drawbacks," which is to say, if you channel all your energy into sports, you risk a harsh transition when your career is over.

For Hess, the transition was eventually eased by the life she has built with her husband and three young kids, as well as a growing counseling practice in which her clients cover a wide spectrum—kids, men and women at marital crossroads, even high-level athletes. In Jon Hess's eyes, Sara's commitment is in part a function of her competitive nature. She had to excel at *something*, and this was the next thing. But it also couldn't be just anything, because it was evident she had an ability to connect with people who find themselves familiarly adrift.

"I see her really trying to identify with their struggles," Jon says. "I think the fact that she's been on their side of the couch trying to deal with issues of identity makes her receive the benefit of the doubt."

I ask Sara how much of her story she shares with her clients. She says she shares if they ask. There's a brief reference to her soccer career on her website, but otherwise the remnants of her past only emerge in how she approaches each problem.

"Certainly putting everything into it—the very humbling National Team experience, the misery of the Olympic experience, the complete medical trauma, and the deep depression followed by the eating disorder stuff and self-loathing—taking all of that, not only does it increase my sense of empathy, I think the relatability to people who walk into my office has been incredibly successful quicker," she says. "It doesn't take two months to establish a rapport. I get them, and I think they trust me in a way that's different."

What we'll never know is what life would have been like for Hess if things had gone more smoothly. Suppose her stint on the National Team had continued on its upward trajectory. Suppose she never got hurt and she stopped playing when she wanted and thus wasn't forced to contend with all the complicated emotions that arise from the abrupt end to a career. There probably wouldn't be occasion for her to sit across the table from me telling me her story. And she wouldn't be pointing to her right leg, to a collection of scars around her knee, and then to a tattoo of Chinese letters on her ankle that mean "Good things come out of chaos." Hess could have had an easier road, but it's doubtful she would have emerged from it as strong as she is today.

Two decades after she was part of history at the Rose Bowl, Hess can celebrate a more remarkable victory in how she didn't let negative outcomes fester and instead channeled the experience into something productive. In enduring the end of her soccer career and the medical saga that followed, she was a prime candidate for "Why bother?" thinking, when the inclination is to throw up your hands and lament all the ways you've been cheated. Instead, in the same way she pushed herself to run through her tears, Hess recognized it fell to her to steer herself through her lowest moments. Given enough time, she came to embrace the notion that your worst moments and your most important moments can often be the same thing.

"I wonder what I would have learned had I not gone through all this stuff," she tells me. "Probably not much."

8

"My Startup Failed. Fuck.": The Surprising Profits in Bankruptcy

*There is no disgrace in honest failure; there is disgrace in fearing to fail.
What is past is useful only as it suggests ways and means for progress.*
—HENRY FORD

JORDAN NEMROW SAW dollar signs. He had an idea that couldn't miss. When Nemrow, fresh out of college, thought about the launch of his startup, he figured it wouldn't take long for his life to change. Six months, he thought. Maybe a year.

This was in 2010—not long after the release of the movie *The Social Network*, about Facebook founder Mark Zuckerberg—and Nemrow found himself watching the film often as some sort of reference for how life as a successful technology entrepreneur might unfold.

"I remember thinking, 'I can't believe this idea doesn't exist,'" Nemrow tells me. "'There's no way it can fail. It's the best idea in the world.'"

Nemrow and his partner, Dan Polaske, called their startup Zillionears. It was a flash sale site designed to let musicians sell their music directly to their fans. The more people who bought an album, the more the price would get driven down, all based on a dynamic pricing model Nemrow conceived. Nemrow figured people on both ends of the transaction would flock to the website—musicians wanting to bypass retailers like Apple, fans wanting to get music at reduced rates. When Nemrow and Polaske floated the concept to a few friends and family members, the reception was positive.

As months passed and Nemrow and his small company hacked away to perfect Zillionears before launch, this feedback was what they were going on. They talked to very few musicians. They spent countless hours on the placement of buttons and other frivolous design features. Even when Polaske mentioned in passing that he couldn't ever see himself using a product like Zillionears, the team never really thought twice.

"We kind of just turned our heads the other way to that," Nemrow says. "We saw our destiny. To me it was going to change the face of not just music, but commerce. I thought, 'I'm going to change everyone's shopping behavior.' And then as time goes on you realize that changing user behavior is not going to happen."

When Zillionears launched, it was a bust for all sorts of reasons. The company had problems collecting payments from consumers. The few artists who participated were confused by the business model. But most of all, people didn't really like it or need it. Before long, Nemrow found himself on the phone with Polaske while walking in a park near his parents' house. He still lived at home, which is how he could survive working at a business that made no money. The conversation felt like an overdue breakup call with a girlfriend, the two men trying to circumvent the awkward reality staring them in the face.

"Eventually I said, 'We should take this thing behind the barn and shoot it in the head,'" Nemrow says. "He said OK, and that was it."

As painful conversations go, there's one like it in Silicon Valley pretty much every day.

THE FAILED STARTUP entrepreneur is as much a cliché now as the out-of-work actor waiting tables. Everyone knows one, or at least has heard of one. According to Professor Shikhar Ghosh, who teaches entrepreneurship at Harvard Business School, about 75 percent of startups don't make money back for investors. The reasons for failure vary, but as he puts it, most "commit suicide as opposed to being murdered"—the damage is usually self-inflicted.

"Probably the biggest single reason startups fail is they create services that not enough people want," Ghosh says. "A subcategory of that is a business people are interested in, but not interested enough to part with their money or time."

A study by the market research firm CB Insights arrived at similar findings. In reviewing the postmortems of 135 failed startups, the firm constructed a list of twenty reasons startups fail, with everything from burnout to location cited. By far the biggest reason was "not arriving at a market need."

This dilemma calls to mind the annual PGA Merchandise Show I attend in Orlando. It's the biggest trade show in golf, with a convention center the size of a small city filled with everything from golf clubs to sweaters to a hundred little gadgets that might allow you to monogram your golf tees. The best description of the PGA show came from my friend and colleague David Owen, who said many of the golf products there are "solutions to problems you didn't know existed." I've found myself walking across that showroom floor dozens of times chuckling at one far-fetched idea or another. It's less funny when I remember someone put all kinds of time, money, and hope into something no one really wants.

As Professor Ghosh says, the most common mistake made with a startup is in miscalculating a product's potential. It's assuming that there are scores of golfers who want their initials printed on a golf tee, or that artists will be lining up for new ways to sell their music. From there, the dominos fall. Entrepreneurs might oversell the idea to investors. Or they inflate internal expectations of what the endeavor will yield. They spend too much time tinkering with a product to get it to work, and not enough time constructing a plan for if it doesn't. The list of ways you can screw up a startup is long enough to cover several semesters at Harvard. And while no one plans it this way, many who emerge from the depths of a failed business tend to be better off from the experience.

"What I see among entrepreneurs who fail or experience setbacks is that the most resilient of them look at it as a learning opportunity and they grow from it," says Dr. Michael Freeman, a psychiatrist in the Bay Area who works with many failed entrepreneurs. "They're able to constructively reflect on it as a way to develop new skills."

In perhaps no other segment of American culture is failure embraced as freely as in the tech industry, where a collapsed startup is rarely a stigma and can often be a credential. It sounds like an odd thing to say about a field so ruthlessly competitive. Yet it is because innovation is inherently paired with risk that mistakes are considered inevitable. The only way to know if a product works is to test it, even if it means subjecting oneself to disapproval. The popular Silicon Valley mantra "Fail fast" reflects a culture that encourages individuals to throw ideas against a wall, then move on if they don't stick.

"It's like what Thomas Edison said: 'I have not failed, I've just found ten thousand ways that won't work,'" Freeman says. "That's sort of the mentality you need to have."

Edison was ahead of his time in embracing the concept of the microfailure, which is the idea that small setbacks are unavoidable and, as a result, shouldn't be feared. When Dr. Jonathan Fader works with major league baseball players, he reminds them that even the best players make an out two out of every three times at the plate, which should temper the disappointment of a pop fly to center field. "Instead of thinking of it as a global definition of yourself, you think of it as an occurrence," Fader says. "A microfailure describes an instance. It doesn't describe the person."

A failed business in Silicon Valley should be viewed in

the same light. It's a swing and a miss as opposed to some larger commentary on your competence. Recognizing as much can be elusive since it's hard not to wrap your self-worth up in something that is consuming your existence. But it helps to know that in the tech world, a lot more people are making outs than getting on base.

WHAT GOOD CAN come when your idea blows up in your face? That's something Jordan Nemrow was forced to contemplate.

At least in his case, his business was self-funded. He lived at home. For a while, he even juggled a desk job that allowed him to hack away at Zillionears on the other company's time. The investment, at least financially, was relatively low.

The risk was in the emotional stake he placed in a company that he thought was going to make him famous. What followed its collapse was the expected dose of humiliation and anxiety, then the postmortems in which he started to recognize his mistakes. He wrote a blog post entitled "My Startup Failed. Fuck." With more than one hundred thousand views, it ended up being by far the most popular thing to arise from Zillionears.

"I kind of wanted to see visually what I had accomplished in eighteen months," Nemrow says. "I wasn't thinking there'd be any positives, but when I wrote it I felt like I actually could do another startup. I have so much knowledge based on things we did wrong."

To recognize that a startup failure can yield an after-life is the next best thing to your business succeeding. And it's not as distant a second as you'd think. For Nemrow, his experience from Zillionears led to a job at a venture called Teleborder where they were specifically looking for engineers with failed startup experience. "It helps building out products because you know what doesn't work," he says.

At Teleborder, Nemrow met an aspiring entrepreneur named Trey Griffith who had a similar story. Griffith, too, had attempted a startup shortly after college. His, too, fell flat. In some ways, their experiences were similar—the wide-reaching ideation phase, the endless tinkering, the sobering realization that whatever they were doing wasn't working. But Griffith's perspective was plenty different. He and his partners started their company, Endorse.me, as more of a type of social network, but they quickly decided the idea was better served as a job marketplace for recent college graduates looking to showcase themselves to potential employers. Plus, Griffith had the more traditional startup experience of trying to land—and then answer to—investors.

Fund-raising for a startup is vital if you're (a) not bringing in any revenue and (b) not in a position to live with your parents. It's also intensely stressful because there's a tendency to spend more time trying to keep the lights on at a business than executing the company's vision. Adding to the stress is the prospect that you're not only failing yourself but whoever's writing you checks.

"Before we raised money, a lot of the focus was raising money. And then you're working on the product basically to raise more money," Griffith says. "It's a common problem."

To start, Griffith and his partners had secured investors from the East Coast who enabled the Endorse.me team to rent some modest office space, eat Subway for lunch, and take economy flights to meet with potential partners. But there was still no money coming in. When he traveled to visit with various companies to gauge whether they'd utilize his product—and more important, whether they'd pay to do so—he got a lot of maybes but rarely a solid yes. The more time passed without any validation of their product, the more their reserves dwindled, the more they started to question whether it was worth continuing.

"It's really hard to know whether you have a successful product unless you definitely have one," Griffith says. "It didn't feel like we struck anything. It didn't feel like people were responding to our idea. I think we had something, but we probably went after the wrong customer, but by then I had invested a year and a half and we were running out of money."

Many startup founders talk about the importance of knowing when exactly to shut down their business, which, as skills go, is a rather morbid one to have. In the CB Insights study listing reasons startups fail, this is listed as "failing to pivot when necessary." The thinking is that the quicker you abandon a flawed idea, the quicker you can move onto something better. Timing is vital, but there often remains this nagging sense you could be giving up too early, which is a reflection of the type of internal drive that makes one an entrepreneur in the first place.

The author Napoleon Hill wrote of a prospector who spent months digging for gold, then gave up and sold his equipment to a junk man. The junk man made millions when he discovered there was a vein of gold three feet from where the prospector had stopped digging.

The cautionary tale lives on in California centuries later. "You always feel like the answer is under the next rock," Griffith says.

The modern-day version of Hill's story might be found in Tim Westergren, the founder of the Internet radio company Pandora, who maxed out eleven credit cards and made unsuccessful pitches to 347 investors before he finally connected with number 348. It was the next $9 million of funding that helped turn the company into a success. "We could tell he was an entrepreneur who wasn't going to fail," the venture capitalist Larry Marcus said about why he chose to invest with Westergren.

But there is a fine line between being persistent and being a fool, and for every Pandora story, there are scores of entrepreneurs who cling to their idea too long in part because they don't want to face being wrong. In other fields, stubborn determination like Westergren's is a signal of character. In the tech world, it takes more courage to know when to pull the plug.

"People who are more self-aware and are willing to fail in small ways have a much higher likelihood of success,"

Ghosh says. "The problem is with those people who are so afraid of failing because they've put everything into an idea, when they would have been better off pivoting away and trying something else."

When it came time for Griffith and his partners to shut down Endorse.me, the emotional toll of seeing the business flame out was deep, and he went through a period when he struggled with seeing any positives at all. What helped was the eventual recognition that he had plenty of company, and that what he had attempted was exceedingly hard. Even better was when prospective employers saw the merits in his experience as well.

"I got my next job because I had proven I could build a product," he says. "From a reputation standpoint, having your own startup signals that you're OK with ambiguity. You're not afraid to get your hands dirty. In a startup you kind of do everything so you kind of go through a boot camp in marketing and product development."

The lessons he had learned were profound enough that when Griffith found himself on the other end of interviews, sitting across from job candidates, he gravitated toward those who had been through similar trials. But that alone wasn't enough. When Griffith asked candidates who had failed startups what they could have done better, he was looking for thoughtful, detailed answers, which many interviewees were able to provide. But there were also those who were reluctant to take ownership of their role in the company's downfall, always citing the errors of others instead. Those stories, Griffith says, "raised a red flag. It shows me that they didn't have a great awareness of their company or their role in it."

As with other failures, the appeal is not the failure itself, but the growth that might result from it. Nemrow's and Griffith's Silicon Valley stories are instructive not just because they endured the hardship of a good idea collapsing around them, but because they emerged from the ordeal stronger than when they started. All over the valley are entrepreneurs who have banked valuable knowledge about starting a business, all stemming from their inability to do so. Some come away from the ordeal with their next idea. The most fortunate, like my friend Ian Shea, arrive at a better understanding of themselves.

OF MY OLDEST and closest friends, no one projects more confidence than Ian Shea. There are guys in our tight group who make plenty more money, and many of us are blessed to have houses and wives and kids. But even in the absence of these traditional benchmarks, Ian has always seemed to float above the fray. Tall and broad, with perpetual stubble, Ian is not a bachelor for lack of options; I've experienced many times the curious phenomenon of walking into a bar and drawing extended glances from random women—only to realize they're all looking at him. Women love Ian, but his appeal is wider than that. Guys are drawn to Ian. My kids love Ian. He is what Malcolm Gladwell, in his book *The Tipping Point*, describes as a connector.

The oldest of five kids, Ian revealed his entrepreneurial streak early, and it was apparent his ability to galvanize others would serve him. When he was ten, he led a group of friends in canvassing the neighborhood to shovel driveways for money. When we shared a house on Martha's Vineyard one summer in college, I was his employee in the window cleaning company he started. Back at Cornell the following fall, he launched a catering service that made a small killing. Although he landed a job in investment banking right out of school and then moved west to work for a tech company, ReplayTV, there was little doubt Ian would branch off on his own once he found the right outlet for his ambition and charisma.

"I knew I wanted to start a business, but I wanted to do it from scratch, and I wanted to be in the best position to do it," he tells me.

By 2009, having lived in San Francisco for nearly a decade, Ian was still looking for the right idea to launch a business around. Everyone else seemed to have one, and it gnawed at him that he wasn't there. Then one night he found himself at a dinner with Scot Schmidt, a professional skier and a star of dozens of extreme skiing videos, who told Ian he often fielded requests for advice from recreational skiers. They wanted to consult in person, or even on the phone. The seeds of an idea started to germinate. What if there was a simple way for people to access authorities in a chosen field? Ian thought of a site that could be an "eBay for experts," where the average person could be put in contact with a wide swath of people with specific knowledge or expertise, and pay for their time. The more Ian thought about it, the more he sensed an opportunity. "Academically, it held water," he says.

When Ian began pitching investors on his startup, now called Maestro Market, he sold them on his vision of a company that could connect people in meaningful ways. He secured money from a host of investors, including family and some of our good friends who had fared well on Wall Street (he knew better than to ask his buddy scraping by on a journalist's salary). Wisely, he steered clear of making promises of big financial returns.

"You never go in saying this is going to be a billion-dollar company. You say this is going to be meaningful," he says. "The emphasis is behind the meaning of what you're doing, and once that resonates, the person is either going to write you a check or not."

Entrepreneurs often talk about the need for validation in its various forms. Hearing people like your idea is one kind of validation. Raising capital is another. Landing partners, hiring talent—in the absence of the traditional indicators that say your business is working (namely revenue), this is what you go on. The early days of Maestro Market had this. Ian raised more than $2 million from investors. He hired a talented team of engineers to build out his product. He forged some early partnerships. The other phrase for these sorts of check marks in the tech world is "social proof." Ian had plenty of social proof.

What he never seemed to have enough of was money. The growing concern was that Maestro lacked a specific focus; the site as then constructed was trying to be everything to everyone, which usually means being nothing to no one. In Silicon Valley they call this trying to "boil the ocean"; covering an expanse so vast is untenable, so the real way to make progress is to attack something smaller.

In conversations about sectors of experts the company should target, the team batted around a host of options. Parenting, social media, careers. Ian even came to present to my boss and me at Condé Nast headquarters to see if the publishing giant could somehow be involved. There were plenty of avenues discussed, and Ian was intrigued by some more than others, but he knew the company needed *something*. Plus, with money running low, he thought Maestro could benefit from an A-list partner who could lift the company's visibility. He wrote a series of handwritten letters to an array of influencers, from Oprah Winfrey to Phil Jackson to Apple's Jony Ive, and he heard back from one, a well-known career advice blogger named Penelope Trunk. Trunk, who had already launched a handful of startups, called Ian as he was sitting in a pitch meeting in Houston. She said she was taken by his note and his idea and wanted to talk more about partnering. They spent three hours talking on the phone that night. This was another form of validation, and Ian and his team were energized by the prospect of leveraging Trunk's celebrity into greater growth for Maestro.

Soon Ian was on a plane to Wisconsin to visit with Trunk, who lived there with her family. In their conversations over several days, the two discussed positioning

Maestro as an outlet for connecting people with career experts like her. Ian was excited that the site had found a direction, and with money from the initial round of funding running out, he was armed with a new story to tell investors. "It was a big jolt, because now we've got a focus. Now we've got a person with name recognition," he recalls. "Things were on the up. We were beginning to see daylight." Over the ensuing four months, Ian and Trunk hammered out the details of a partnership, and investors appeared ready to back it.

One Friday in early August, weeks before his fortieth birthday, Ian was preparing to go to New York to put the final touches on the deal that would push the restructured company forward. Maestro was out of money and racking up debt, so the New York trip was a lifeline at just the right time. But before he left, he received a call from one of the investors.

"He said, 'Don't get on the plane. We hate to part ways, but we're parting ways,'" Ian recalls.

The conversation was quick, but it was enough to turn Ian's world upside down. What became apparent is the New York meetings would happen, but with Trunk only. He and his staff were being squeezed out. With the IRS starting to call, Ian arrived at Maestro's headquarters the following Monday with no money to pay his staff, and without a plan.

It was, Ian says, "the most traumatic experience of my life." He also says it was the best thing that could have happened.

*   *   *

MORE THAN THE average guy, Ian has always been attuned to his physical and emotional wellness. That's not a phrase we would have used back in high school. More like, we'd all be ready to go out for the night when Shea, that flake, would decide he first needed a two-hour nap. Regardless, it's always been a part of him. Getting in a good workout, eating right, building in sufficient time to "relax"—these were all things that mattered to Ian and which the rest of us used to poke fun at to no end. A story we still tell today involves our high school's volatile football coach, who exploded at Ian one day for missing a block in practice. Ian's response was that the coach shouldn't stress so much. "It's not the end of the world, Coach," he said. This is always how he's operated, and as time has passed and the stress in our lives has heightened, Ian's focus on his well-being has only grown more acute.

A couple of years before starting Maestro Market, after breaking up with a woman he thought he was going to marry, Ian started working with a spiritual counselor named Dr. DiVanna Vadree. The breakup was intensely painful, and he wanted to better manage his emotions, so Vadree taught Ian breathing techniques and meditation. Vadree, who is based outside Seattle, describes her work as focusing on "energy and consciousness with a spiritual base." Her emphasis is on helping clients connect with their spirit by stripping out all the counterproductive workings of our mind—anxiety, fear, negativity. "It's about a depth of surrender," Vadree tells me. "When you commit at a deeper level, you are calling forth a different energy than someone who is just going with the tide."

The fact that Ian had gravitated toward someone like Vadree wasn't a complete surprise. Ribbing aside, I think everyone in our group of friends admires the way he lives his life by a code he defines. But I could see why, when it came time for Maestro to pick a focus, the concept of wellness never came up.

"None of the things we were looking at for Maestro were things I was dialed into personally," Ian says. "Here I was heavily into this emotional and spiritual practice, but I didn't let anybody know about it. I was ashamed or embarrassed, whatever you want to call it."

The first reason that Maestro's implosion proved to be so beneficial to Ian is it prevented him from going down a path he wasn't fully prepared to travel. Think of it as a bad marriage. If your heart's not really in it, you're not doing anyone any favors by keeping it to yourself. As much as Ian believed in the general idea of Maestro, the focus on something he wasn't deeply passionate about would have been a missed opportunity. That's not to suggest we all need to choose work that thrills us; otherwise, there'd be no one to sell us life insurance. But there's a danger in stifling your true self, particularly in an endeavor where an emotional investment is such a vital component. If you recall Abraham Maslow's "hierarchy of needs," the last vital part is self-actualization, in which you're doing what you're meant to do. Had Maestro succeeded in the way Ian had planned with Trunk, it would have pushed him further from what he came to identify as more meaningful work. Had Maestro succeeded, in fact, he likely wouldn't have come up with a new idea.

"When something falls apart, we retreat and we're confused and we're hurt," Vadree says. "At the spiritual level someone's conscious will say, 'Where was my spirit in this?' But at the end of the day, there was something right about this collapsing. Ian wasn't ready. The maturation of the vision hadn't occurred."

Convenient as it sounds, these sorts of benefits were hardly apparent early. In the months after the collapse of his business, Ian retreated into a type of protective shell. Struggling with what to do next, he consulted often with Vadree. When he holed up in our friend Conor's apartment in New York City for several months, he rarely went out, but he wanted the assurance that the people important to him were at least close. Ian and I have an uncommon relationship. He has long been one of my best friends, but we can go months without being in the same room. I mention this because I grasped only later how trying a period this was for him.

"I got the shit knocked out of me," he says.

When I ask Ian if he could identify a low point, he says it wasn't one pronounced moment, but "an extended period of feeling bad." It was the opposite of validation—the isolation of sitting alone in an apartment when all his friends were at real jobs, the repeated calls from the IRS, explaining everything to his family. According to Dr. Michael

Freeman, the psychiatrist who works with failed entrepreneurs, the two emotions that commonly follow a business collapsing are humiliation and demoralization. Ian became familiar with both, and were it not for his work with Vadree, he says, they could have swallowed him whole.

"When you get the call from the investors saying they are moving on and they've lost faith in you, and then you have to lay off the team, your mind is going to absolutely freak out and say, 'You're a loser. It's all over.' The umpteen stories it will spin," he said. "I think it's very hard without some support to disengage from that and not let that overcome you with panic or fear or worry."

With time, Ian became determined to combat his anxiety. Since Conor was already at work by the time Ian awoke, Ian would spend the first part of the morning meditating. He started keeping a journal and writing down gratitudes. Then he'd watch a TED talk or read. When he ventured out, it was to see speakers on personal growth and spirituality. "These were the things getting me from Monday to Tuesday to Wednesday," he says. At this point, Ian hadn't officially shuttered Maestro Market, and a part of him was still in that startup mode where he felt guilty that he wasn't hunched over a laptop firing off emails. But he also sensed that that wasn't going to deliver what he was after.

"I simplified my life to only things that were nourishing and supportive," he wrote later. "I developed a daily process that helped me stabilize, which included digesting online videos, articles, books and other content sent from trusted people. While absorbing all that, I continually sought out different perspectives by connecting with experts, friends, family and most importantly, myself."

The more Ian opened himself up to this menu of support, the better equipped he was to chip away at his insecurities. He enjoyed exploring his inner self and, in a strange way, came to appreciate feeling vulnerable because he recognized an ability to handle it. Home for dinner with his folks, Ian fielded the inevitable questions about what he planned to do next. There was a gentle push for him to give up on his own business and get a regular job. He was nothing if not employable. But Ian said he was thinking about doing something around spirituality, which, practically speaking, was like saying he was thinking of opening a bed-and-breakfast on the moon.

The way Ian talks about some of this stuff, you half expect him to be wearing a robe and sandals handing out flyers on a street corner. But if you met him, he is a regular guy. He wears T-shirts and sneakers, plays a lot of basketball. The reason this was important is because when it came to issues of wellness, Ian recognized he was accessible. He sensed he could be a bridge between the spiritual world he continued to explore and a wider base of people who approached such topics with trepidation.

Later, Ian came to think of this time as his product development, albeit a highly unconventional product development process. If his mistake with Maestro was arriving at a focus he wasn't passionate about, his response was to now home in on something he lived and breathed. What he sensed was that the type of support he had tapped into existed on the fringes of our society, but there was no mechanism for pulling it into the mainstream. "I realized that what I was going through was no different than what millions of other people go through, whether it's a divorce or having trouble having a child," he says. "There's a reason the self-help industry is a forty-billion-dollar industry, but no one wants to talk about it."

In February 2015, eighteen months after the collapse of Maestro Market, I got an email from Ian, who was ready to reveal what he'd been up to. Attached was a fifteen-page PowerPoint laying out his vision for his new company, I-M-Human, which he billed as a "Revolutionary Support System." At the beginning was Ian's personal story and how the demise of one venture shaped the idea of a site comprising "real, relatable content for inspiration and information." As with his original idea, the new platform would be an outlet for interactions with experts. But it would also be a forum for online sharing, both of users' individual stories and the type of support content that had resonated with Ian in his darkest moments. Deeper in the memo were all kinds of charts and profit and loss projections, and it was apparent that Ian had thought through every aspect of his new venture. As of this writing, he has made early progress fund-raising, has started to assemble a new team of talent and advisers, and has attracted interest from potential partners such as GLAAD and the actress Goldie Hawn's foundation.

Ian is aware uncertainty remains. The vision for I-M-Human is to create the type of nurturing community that social media networks like Facebook and Twitter have fallen short of achieving. The world would be better because of it, and in my biased opinion, Ian has the type of disarming personality that could help remove some of the stigma around emotional support. Says Alta Tseng, who first worked with Ian as a creative consultant but has since joined I-M-Human as a vice president: "I'm Chinese American and it'd be one thing for me to say I want to do something around personal growth. But it's different when it's this tall, good-looking corn-fed ex–finance guy who comes across as very genuine."

Still, I've now had enough conversations about the long odds facing startups to temper my optimism. There's no guarantee I-M-Human won't end up like Zillionears or Endorse.me, tossed onto the scrap heap of can't-miss ideas that are now only discussed in the past tense. For the purposes of this story, though, I'm not sure it really matters. Think back to the skater Dan Jansen faltering in three Olympic races, then spending hours sifting through his disappointments with the help of the psychologist Jim Loehr. By the end, Loehr had helped Jansen accept that the results of his races were secondary to the growth he achieved in preparing for them. The skater's ability to reframe the narrative of his career was a greater breakthrough than the gold medal that followed.

"What is really required is a dedication to the mission. That's more important," Loehr says. "Who you become is a consequence of the chase more than what you accomplished in the chase."

Loehr's point is that a failed venture yields benefits re-gardless of what happens next. There needn't be a "sweep-ing redemptive ending" in the form of a gold medal or an IPO or whatever your measure of success is. Those always make for great stories. But the sheer experience of enduring failure and working through the pain that accompanies it can still make us stronger in ways we can't always quantify.

This is what Ian came to determine. As much as he hopes to parlay the failure of one business into the triumph of another, the more important point is that he emerged from an ordeal on more solid footing. I heard variations of the same thing from Nemrow and Griffith, and in the countless postmortem blog posts written about the close of this business or that. Ian talks about his current existence as if on an x-y axis. With his business still in its frightening formative stages, he is taking on more risk than ever in the form of time, money, and hope. "The danger line has gone up, up, up, but at the same time my fears have only gone down," he says. "Technically you should be pulling me off the ceiling based on the traditional things I should be wor-ried about. But I'm not worried because I've gotten to this point. Maybe I'm delusional. But I don't think so."

9

The Power of Stick-to-itiveness: The Greatest Team That Never Won a Game

Strange how people who suffer together have stronger connections than those who are most content.
—Bob Dylan

Football was not my game. I played for two years, in eighth and ninth grade, and at the very least, the experience confirmed that I shouldn't play much longer.

My problem was that organized football exposed all my athletic inefficiencies at once. I was neither fast, nor strong, nor terribly tough. In the other sports I played, like hockey or baseball, I could circumvent these weaknesses because I had good hands and a decent head for the games, but football is less likely to reward such peripheral talent. I wasn't dynamic enough to play any of the skill positions, so they stuck me on the line, where at 140 pounds I was a slightly more effective blocker than a house plant.

The summer before ninth grade, I had a job mowing a bunch of lawns around town, and I remember telling one homeowner, Mr. Gothberg, that I couldn't tend to his yard the following afternoon. "I have football practice tomorrow," I said. Mr. Gothberg laughed just then, chuckling heartily for several seconds, before asking, "No, seriously, where will you be tomorrow?"

In determining whether I wanted to continue playing football after ninth grade, the calculation was fairly simple. I already knew I wasn't very good, and could sense I wouldn't have much opportunity to play as I progressed through high school. That alone wasn't necessarily a deterrent, but the biggest factor was football wasn't particularly fun. I'd ridden the bench in other sports, but those sports still engaged me through practice. I enjoyed two-on-ones in hockey and shagging flies in baseball. In football, there was just an endless parade of leg lifts and up-downs. When it came to running actual plays, it was only a matter of time before I found myself sprawled on my back.

The following fall, I went out for the school play.

Even as some of my friends went on to enjoy high school football success and the social status that came with it, I never regretted my decision to stop playing. At least not until recently, when I met a former college football player named Nick Leone.

Leone is a few years older than I am and athletically more gifted—strong and quick, but with all those intangible qualities, too. As a high school cornerback in football-mad Florida, he lined up against four wide receivers who were NFL draft picks, and only one, a future Hall of Famer named Michael Irvin, got past him into the end zone.

"So I was good," Leone says almost apologetically.

Of his experience playing football at Columbia Univer-

sity, Leone describes the discipline it required, not to mention the kinship he still feels with his teammates. Recently,
he received an award for distinguished alumni from the
university, and he shared the video of his speech, when
he called out to his college teammates seated at a table in
the back of the room. The table exploded, a collection of
well-lubricated middle-aged men basking in the celebration
of one of their own. The vibe you got from the sequence was
that the group shared a special bond, all stemming from
their triumphant days on the field together. But that's only
partially true. The bond the men shared was indeed deep
and meaningful, and it's now spanned parts of four decades.
Yet the experience that forever linked them was far more
powerful than a collection of winning seasons.

In fact, it was a college football career in which they
didn't win a single game.

THESE CALCULATIONS ABOUT how we invest our time
should be simple. When I stopped playing football, it was
because I didn't find it fun. When Sara Hess left the US
Women's National Team, it was because the experience tore
at her confidence. What's interesting about Nick Leone's
time playing football at Columbia, where the Lions drew
national headlines for losing forty-four straight games, is
that this all applied to him as well. Forget about fun. His
entire college football career was defined by futility. In the
eyes of other Columbia students, the team was a joke. Yet
Leone still showed up every day, and he and his teammates

now talk about their football careers as perhaps the most enriching experience of their lives.

"When I had job interviews after college I never had to bring it up, because with guys it was the first thing they asked about," Leone says. "It was that big a deal. People looked at me and said, 'What was it like to lose for four years?' And I'd say, 'It was a horrible experience, but I played with my best friends. We weren't that good, but I didn't quit and I think I learned a lot.' I think that story impressed people."

Being part of one of the worst college football teams in history was at least a conversation starter. The streak began when Leone and his classmates were seniors in high school. It ended when they were out of college and into the workforce. In between were blowouts and late collapses, three different head coaches, and dozens of players who couldn't take the losing and quit. Only twelve players who started together in freshman football were still there as seniors. Those were the men whooping and hollering during Leone's speech, a band of survivors who resented every minute of the losing but have learned to embrace it in the years since.

"Look at how many lawyers and doctors we have," says Matt Sodl, an All-Ivy selection at defensive tackle and now a hedge fund manager. "A lot of it goes back to what we went through. When you're really faced with adversity, it crafts how you think, how you look at certain situations, and how you analyze problems."

It went beyond the typical Ivy League education. For

several years after college, Leone was active mentoring current members of the football team in their search for jobs. In that time, the Lions continued to struggle, 1–9 one season, 2–8 the next. "But the kids were still there every day, and they had the right attitude and the right goals," Leone says. By the time the seniors sat down for the annual spring football dinner, many had lucrative jobs lined up on Wall Street and elsewhere.

A few years passed. Leone went to another spring football dinner with a collection of seniors weeks from graduation. This time only one had a job secured, and a fairly unimpressive one at that.

What was the difference? I ask.

"They went 8–2," he says.

"I'm not saying you can't have one without the other," he continues. "But from my standpoint, when you spend four years with people laughing at you, you maybe come away with a little more hunger."

The point isn't that a player who is successful at football is bound to flounder elsewhere. But Leone says the trials of his losing football career were a vital part of his education. They helped harden him in ways that might not have happened had his team been simply bad and not awful. He tells the story of his start in finance, when it was common for him to work straight through the night, come home to shower, then head back to the office. In his first five years out of school, he missed the Super Bowl because he was at his desk working. A lesser version of himself wouldn't have lasted a week, but Leone says his resilience traces to what he calls his "uncoddling" phase at Columbia, when he realized his best effort wasn't enough, and no one was there to soften the blow. Every loss still resulted in unsparing headlines in the New York papers, and it still resulted in football players getting mocked by other students as they walked across campus. That he looks at the time now as a gift is a function of perspective and maturity. But it's not what any of them were hoping for when they first moved into their dorms.

You don't pick Columbia if your primary objective is to win football games. The campus is located just shy of Harlem in northern Manhattan, but the football field is another twenty minutes up the line, so players need to ride a bus each day to and from practice. The Columbia Lions' last Ivy League title was in 1961. By the time the class of 1988 entered school as freshmen, the program had won one game in each of the previous five years and hadn't had a winning season since 1972.

So those who committed to play were not under any grand illusions. But they still went in regarding football as more than an extracurricular diversion. Many of the core players in the class of 1988 were accomplished high school athletes. Leone was a three-sport standout in Pompano Beach, Florida. Quarterback David Putelo was fresh off helping to turn a beleaguered program at Long Island's Malverne High School into a winning team. Matt Sodl came out of a powerhouse in rural Pennsylvania that sent more than a dozen players to Division I programs. These new Columbia players had options at other Ivy League schools but were intrigued by going to a prestigious institution in the heart of New York City, with the added prospect of helping to reverse a program's fortunes.

"Nobody picks a college and says 'I'm going to go and lose a lot of games,'" Putelo says. "I knew Columbia wasn't a great or storied program, but you envision going there and making an impact."

In the early stages especially, there was reason to be hopeful. In January 1985, Columbia hired a new head coach, Jim Garrett, who arrived with extensive experience in the NFL and three sons who could help the Lions win. One son, John, was already playing at Columbia. Another, Jason, was a star freshman quarterback at Princeton who transferred to Columbia to play under his father (and later went on to coach the Dallas Cowboys). A third, Judd, was a prized high school recruit who would enroll alongside his brothers. For Ivy League football, the Garretts were difference makers. The other players could see it when all three were on the field in practice (although NCAA rules allowed only John, already a Columbia student, to play that first year). And the dad . . . well, the dad was hard-core.

In the weeks leading up to Garrett's first season, the coach put the team through a rigorous training camp that was unlike anything Columbia football had experienced before, with multiple-session days that amounted to thirty-three practices in less than two weeks. Like something out of the movie *Remember the Titans*, Garrett's practices would run so late the coaching staff gathered cars around the field so headlights would illuminate the action. John Miller, the starting center, remembers needing to patch up the bottoms of his feet with tape because they were worn through with blisters. "I can't tell you how many conversations I had with my dad telling him how hard it was," Miller says. For a time, though, it seemed worth it because Garrett had infused them all with faith.

"From the first meeting we had with this coach, he had us convinced we were going to go 10–0," Leone says. "And literally everyone believed him."

The momentum carried into the Lions' first game against Harvard, the two-time defending Ivy League champion. For the sophomores like Leone, it was their first varsity game, and they seemed poised to deliver on Garrett's bluster. At halftime the Lions were up 17–0.

"We were all going crazy," Matt Sodl recalls. "We're banging our heads against the locker, and the coach says, 'I can see it in the *New York Times*: Columbia Shocks the World!'"

Well, there were headlines at least. When the Crimson scored their first touchdown in the third quarter to get within ten, a mild panic fluttered through the Columbia sidelines, players all reflexively looking at the scoreboard in hopes that time was elapsing quickly. It was like Greg Norman making that opening bogey in the final round of the Masters, the first cloud of an approaching storm. Then Harvard scored again. And then again. When players filed off the field, the final score was Harvard 49, Columbia 17, and Garrett was left to make sense of how this seemingly battle-ready group had been blown over by the first breath of resistance. His legacy as a coach will be forever tied to what he said next.

"They are drug-addicted losers," Garrett famously told the press. "One adversity comes and bang! They're right back in the sewer again."

Especially by Ivy League standards, it was a rich metaphor. Garrett's point was that losing had become ingrained in his players' subconscious. More than what a handful of fiery speeches and marathon practices could counter, it was a problem that existed almost at a molecular level. But nuance doesn't make for great headlines, and Garrett didn't help himself by laying into punter Pete Murphy, who he said performed so poorly under pressure that he'd have a hard time holding down a job after college. "I want to see him when he graduates and goes to work downtown on Wall Street and does three things that he did today. See how long he is gonna work for that company, how long Merrill Lynch or Smith Barney is gonna have him around." (Garrett was at least right about Murphy never getting a job on Wall Street. He became a successful doctor instead.)

The fallout from Garrett's outburst was immediate. The New York papers all pounced on his comments, and the university administration was quick to reprimand him as well. The coach spent much of the year trying to apologize, but the damage was done, and the losses continued to pile up like snow on a parked car. At the end of his 0–10 campaign, Garrett was shown the door, with his sons all transferring to Princeton. Almost everyone agreed Garrett was a sophisticated football mind, but his style was ill-suited for the Ivy League, and his locker-room diatribe about Columbia's losing culture was just an example.

What fewer have ventured to discuss is whether the old coach was actually right.

THE MOST DESTRUCTIVE type of losing is the kind that feeds off itself. Simply put, it's that dynamic where because you lost today, you're more likely to lose again tomorrow. I could fill pages of this book—not to mention hours of a therapist's schedule—with the details of my misadventures on the tennis court. (Don't worry, I won't.) But let's just say that because I've lost in so many disheartening ways, a part of me expects to lose again. And so I do.

"Sam's crazy," my wife likes to say when discussing my tennis. I would love to disagree.

Part of what I contend with on the court is what psychologists call a "negativity bias," which is when our brains are wired to focus more on bad things than good. When we talk about losing feeding off itself, this is a big reason. In the tennis matches I lose, for instance, I still win plenty of points. And even in the points I lose, I might hit four pretty good shots before sailing a final forehand long. That one errant forehand is a mere microfailure. It happens to all of us, and I should be quick to dismiss it, yet it invariably ends up being the thing I dwell on most. By succumbing to this negativity bias, I tend to let bad thoughts take over, and from there, I feel as though I'm fated to lose.

With this as an explanation, perhaps it makes sense that Columbia players were rattled as soon as Harvard scored its first touchdown. Sure, they still had a ten-point lead, but there was too much scar tissue between them for anyone to feel secure. Did that make them "drug-addicted losers"? No. But it did make them a team composed of fragile psyches, where even small setbacks tended to fester. And lest you think the team just needed a pep talk and a matinee showing of *Rocky*, you should know the reaction was probably rooted deeper than you think.

Consider that concept of a negativity bias, in which we remember more bad than good. One theory for how we got that way is that it was once vital to our survival; we needed it to remind us of trouble. Walk down a path that leads to a steep drop-off and a broken ankle, and you'll be sure to remember that path the next time. Eat berries that make you violently ill, and you'll remember not to eat those berries again. The need for this bias isn't completely outdated. My son Will's nut allergy has landed him in the hospital twice, including once when he ate a cookie with walnuts, then was stabbed with an EpiPen and carted off in an ambulance. The trauma from that experience is the reason he never puts anything in his mouth without checking the label. Of the countless foods Will has eaten in his life, it is one cookie that has had the most lasting impact.

Dr. Rick Hanson—a psychologist at the University of California, Berkeley, and an author—has described our negativity bias as essentially the difference between remembering "the carrot or the stick," where the fear of danger is stronger than the allure of the reward. "If you miss out on a carrot today, you'll have a chance at more carrots tomorrow," Hanson writes. "But if you fail to avoid a stick today—WHAP!—no more carrots forever. Compared to carrots, sticks usually have more urgency and impact."

At some point in our evolution, experts say, the need to fixate on the unpleasant lost some of its urgency. In some instances it became a hindrance. The sports psychiatrist Dr. Michael Lardon points out that "biological evolution takes thousands upon thousands of years, but sociological evolution takes much less." There's a chance we've outgrown some of our uses for a negativity bias, but like buying a house with a big, ugly TV antenna, we're stuck with it regardless. Perhaps there will come a time when humans can subconsciously distinguish between *real* danger and just blowing a halftime lead in a football game. Until then, one of our ongoing challenges is the way negative thoughts conspire against us at the worst possible times. In his indelicate way, this is what Garrett was saying about his team that Saturday years ago.

"When he proceeded to call us drug-addicted losers, I understood what he was saying," quarterback David Putelo says. "Losing was the drug that we fell back to. We'd be up against Dartmouth or Brown, and then something would happen and they'd score, and we'd be like, 'Here we go again.'"

The fact that our negative thoughts tend to loom large in our heads allows for a greater appreciation of those who possess powerful self-belief. What distinguished Roger

Federer at his peak as the premier player in tennis was not just his sublime strokes but his ability to pull off the big points. Did Federer *always* win them? No. But he convinced himself that he should and thus often did. Same goes for Tiger Woods, who prior to his downfall had an almost divine ability to sink putts when they really mattered. Look at the putt Woods holed to force a playoff in the 2008 US Open, a tournament he went on to win the next day. The putt was downhill and fifteen feet away. One of the great misconceptions about Woods at the height of his powers was that he never missed those putts, which is ridiculous. Woods missed those putts all the time. On the PGA Tour, the best putters make less than one out of three from such a distance. The difference is at crucial moments like this one, Woods had a gift for shutting out his history of misses and converting.

To understand the power of negative thoughts is to know how easy it is to turn microfailures into just failures. The Columbia football players, meanwhile, present an interesting case study. In some ways, as Garrett suggested, they are a classic example of how a negative experience can compound itself, one loss spilling into the next. Only later could they see the losing in an entirely new light.

COLUMBIA'S FOOTBALL PROBLEMS were not limited to a lack of confidence. The talent disparity was real. Recruiting, owing to the school's limited facilities and losing history, was an annual challenge, and even those who did sign on to play had a hard time sticking around. When Jim Garrett took his team to training camp that first August, he loaded three buses full of players and predicted they'd barely need two buses on the way back. He was right.

"And it's not like just the crummy players quit," says Mike Lavelle, a wide receiver and running back on the class of 1988 team. "There were guys who quit who you'd be playing basketball with in the winter and you could see they were these amazing athletes. It felt like we were always saying, 'Imagine if we still had him.'"

"It hurt even more when you were walking around campus and you saw guys who quit in September who'd say, 'Wow, you guys lost again,'" says center John Miller. "It was hard not to want to punch those guys in the face."

Each year at training camp the remaining players would look around, and they'd notice another collection of players gone, with more disappearing from the roster over the course of the fall. To the rest of them, it seemed like a test, a dare to see who would go next. But by then their decision was made. Looking back, there was a common thread through those who went the distance, most of them hailing from working-class backgrounds, all of them feeling fortunate to be at Columbia at all. "You look at all our parents, there weren't a lot of white collars in that group," Miller says.

Mike Lavelle was two weeks away from leaving for school for his freshman year when his father died from leukemia. There was no life insurance, and Mike questioned if he should still go. His mother convinced him he should, and though Lavelle qualified for financial assistance (the

Ivy League doesn't award athletic scholarships), he still emptied most of the family's bank account in order to cover all his costs.

"My mother never saw me play football," he says. "She couldn't because she always had to work."

One thing money allows for is options, and in many players' eyes, football was wrapped up in their arrangement with the school. It was part of what brought them there, and as they saw it even then, what would open doors for them when it was time to leave. When Leone was a high school senior on his recruiting trip to Columbia, he was brought to a football party where his host pointed out the captain of the team in the corner of the room.

"And the only thing my host said about him—he didn't say that he benches three hundred pounds or how much he squats—the only thing he said was, 'That guy's going to work at Salomon Brothers,'" Leone recalls. "I'm this eighteen-year-old kid from Florida and had no idea what that was, but I could tell it was impressive. So when I got to Columbia, I was pretty serious that I'm not going to screw up this opportunity."

Leone's way of weathering the losing was to view it as a means to an end. He hated getting blown out and resented the condescending remarks from other students on campus, but like Michael Dukakis, he was a pragmatist. He saw value in the process and even goes so far as to say that if the team had won no games or three games, it wouldn't have mattered.

"Really?" I ask.

"I'm totally serious." he says. "Maybe in hindsight after thirty years and so much time has passed I'm downplaying how painful it was. But as I sit here today I don't think it would have made much difference. I still would have chosen Columbia. I think for some of the more intense guys, the losing really got to them, and I know I tried just as hard as those guys. But at some point I feel like I got numb to it."

No one loses the same way—from Leone, who grudgingly learned to accept the team's fate; to Putelo, the quarterback who faced the added indignity of getting pulled from games when things got ugly; to a player like Matt Sodl, the Lions' best player and an All-Ivy selection, who tried to squeeze as much as he could out of every game and still came up empty.

In the fall of 1987, the Lions were trailed by cameras from NFL Films, which had latched onto the team's struggle to win a single game. The final product is vintage NFL Films—the full orchestra soundtrack, the dramatic narration, the slow-motion footage that seems to turn every play into a battle between good and evil. You almost could forget that the team featured was one of the worst in college football history. At the center of it is Sodl, ripping past offensive linemen to stop a runner in the backfield, staring intently in the locker room in the minutes before game time.

"Every time my wife watches that video she cries because she knows how much it meant to me," Sodl says.

As much as the loss to Harvard their sophomore year was a media spectacle, it wasn't the most painful. When you give up seven consecutive touchdowns, you're at least allowed time to get used to the idea. Far worse was a game senior year against Dartmouth, when the Lions held a one-point lead in the fourth quarter only to have Dartmouth drive sixty-six yards in the final five minutes, kick a field goal, and go up two. From there, the Lions were allowed one last opportunity—a thirty-nine-yard field goal attempt with nineteen seconds remaining that would have broken a thirty-eight-game losing streak. The kick by Columbia's Kurt Dasbach was "easily long enough," Sodl recalls. "And as I watched it go, I thought, 'Holy man, it's over.'"

But it wasn't. The ball sailed over the uprights but was hooking. Confusion reigned. Columbia's fans stormed the field thinking the Lions had won, but officials waded through the crowd waving no good. The streak lived on. The *New York Times* described the scene of Sodl—the best player on the field, with a hand in sixteen tackles, and this his final home game—trudging to the locker room in tears.

"I have two games left," Sodl told reporters. "And I'll be damned if I go out of here without a win. We have to get psyched up like this every week. We're gonna win."

There would be no win in those games, either. Two weeks later the Lions lost another tight one at Brown, 19–16, and their college careers were over.

"The locker room after that game, I mean the only other time I cried like that was when my dad died," Mike Lavelle says. "Maybe it's just me, but even when we played a team like Penn that was so much better, I was delusional enough to think we could win. And then it was all over, and we never did."

In 2014, a writer named Josh Keefe wrote an essay for *Slate* in which he declared himself "the worst high school quarterback ever." There are no official rankings for this sort of thing, and having covered my share of bad high school football in my newspaper days, I would have enjoyed at least a say in the matter. But there was no sense in quibbling. Bad football is universal in its demoralizing nature, and much of what Keefe described to me is what I experienced in my brief time in the game, and what members of the Columbia team experienced over their four years.

"The thing about football is it's not quite like losing in other sports I've played," Keefe tells me. "I've been on bad baseball teams, but it doesn't really impact you in the same way because in football, rarely are you being beaten badly without being physically dominated. And it's worse at the high school level because you're managing the development of your identity. To throw that big 'L' in the middle of all these swirling hormones was a lot to deal with."

Keefe went to John Bapst Memorial High School in Bangor, Maine, where he took over as the team's quarterback as a sophomore and went 0–23 as a starter. There may be a temptation to say it couldn't have been so bad since he *was* the starting quarterback, which at most schools carries some degree of social currency. Even Columbia players say they could at least enjoy the feeling of walking around campus knowing they were bigger and stronger than most other students. But Keefe says his position carried no cachet. For one thing, he claims he took over only on the strength of two fluky plays his sophomore year—one a long touchdown run during garbage time, when the other team thought he was down; the other a touchdown pass he threw well over the head of his intended receiver, but into the hands of another teammate.

So Keefe didn't feel like he really deserved the job, and then there was the fact that his team was so awful. At his school the dynamic was similar to Columbia in that football was an afterthought. John Bapst was a soccer powerhouse, so Keefe's team tended to attract only the second- and even third-tier athletes. At a fall pep rally for all the school's sports teams, he recalls even the golf team poking fun at them.

"We were a group of misfits," Keefe says. "Even as football players, it was assumed we were the B team."

So Keefe's teams lost and lost big, and much of the experience was predictably miserable. On occasions when a player would be late to the bus taking them to practice, he and his teammates would be grateful for however many minutes they were shaving off practice. When I ask Keefe if he ever came close to quitting, his answer is both noble and honest.

"I probably should have," he says. "But especially as the quarterback, I felt I owed it to everyone to keep playing. I just couldn't. There was this strong allegiance to the rest of the team."

It wasn't just loyalty. Having invested as much as he had already, Keefe was seduced by the prospect of a win and terrified it would happen without him. "Serious FOMO," he says. "I just felt like the payoff would have been huge, like we would have conquered something major."

Instead, like Nick Leone and Matt Sodl, Keefe graduated not knowing a single football win, which led to my inevitable question: What did you learn? He is thirty now, balancing a handful of jobs while also getting his master's degree in journalism. For a while he dabbled in stand-up comedy, and he says his football experience fortified him against the fear of public humiliation.

"I think I learned a lot about the day-to-day grind, about delaying satisfaction," he says. "But it also taught me about owning your failures. You're not going to be able to stay away from it, so better to face it at a young age. I feel like a lot of kids are insulated from failure when they're young, and then they get out of school, and it's a slap in the face."

THE JOURNEY TRAVELED by Keefe and the Columbia players calls to mind David Brooks's book on the development of character, *The Road to Character,* which he begins by describing the difference between "résumé virtues" and "eulogy virtues"—essentially what you'd say about yourself when applying for a job versus what others would say about you at your funeral. The résumé virtues are geared toward our outward skills and accomplishments; the eulogy virtues are the part of our essence that makes us who we are. In his own way, Brooks was describing a dichotomy that is the crux of this book. When we lose, we're often falling short of the conventional type of success we can detail on a piece of paper. But it's also the type of formative experience that will serve us in far more meaningful ways later on.

"Our education system is certainly oriented around the résumé virtues more than the eulogy ones," Brooks writes. "Public conversation is, too—the self-help tips in magazines, the nonfiction best-sellers. Most of us have clearer strategies for how to achieve career success than we do for how to develop a profound character."

The irony of the Columbia football experience is that players went in thinking about it from a résumé perspective. There's no shame in that. These were mostly type A guys who hoped to win some games while forging the connections that would lead to successful careers. "You don't play college football if you're not a competitive guy," says Rich Ritter, a lineman on that team who is now an orthopedic surgeon. The wins never came, but the jobs did. In the group are lawyers and doctors, sales directors and bankers. When Nick Leone was a senior, he was the guy other students talked about who had a multitude of job offers. Yet even then, the most profound impact wasn't where anyone ended up working but the type of men they became and their connections to one another, much of it fostered by the experience of dealing with losing. In other words, the benefits of playing football at Columbia went further toward the development of their eulogy virtues.

In a sadly fitting way, this became apparent at a funeral.

In January 1989, a year after ending his football career without a single win, the Lions' former defensive back Phil Fusco was leaving Hunter Mountain in upstate New York when his Jeep Cherokee hit an icy patch and skidded into a utility pole. Fusco, in his first year of law school at Fordham, was killed instantly. The teammates he left behind were shaken to their core.

"We all leaned on each other pretty hard," John Miller recalls. "To lose a guy when you're twenty-two, in some regards, it was more than we knew how to deal with. There was a unity that we had to force out of each other, but we were closer because of it."

Real tragedy risks rendering any losing streak discussion quite trivial, but Fusco's death was at least reinforcement that their bond would last. Overmatched as teammates on the field, they were committed to one another off it. "When Phil died, it was our first time back together as a group, and it was also the one time we all got together that we didn't think about football," Putelo says. "Phil was a well-loved guy. If we told a story to perk ourselves up, it was a Phil story."

If death belongs in its own category, there were other challenges of postgraduate life players found they were better equipped to handle. You might say this is where they've turned the negativity bias on its head. In the nearly thirty years since their last game, the conversation about their football careers rarely focuses on what went wrong. "I mostly remember the laughs," Putelo says. They cite the fact they've all been married for more than twenty years.

They credit football with helping to shape countless teachable moments with their kids. Professionally, they approach their work with diligence and humility, and with the fortitude to rebound from setbacks.

"I know this isn't a word in the English language, but I call it 'stick-to-itiveness,'" Leone says. "I've been married for twenty years. I've had the same job for the last twenty years. I never once thought about quitting and a lot of people do. But if we went 6–4 or whatever in Columbia and I didn't struggle to the extent that I did, I'm not sure I'd be where I am now."

On the night that he received the John Jay Award for Distinguished Professional Achievement, Leone wore a tuxedo and sat on the dais. An undergraduate student read through his long list of accomplishments in financial restructuring and elsewhere. It was a head-swelling moment, but when it came time for Leone to speak, he was self-effacing. He joked about the boring nature of his job ("Thanks for making it sound interesting"). He referenced the losing football seasons. He thanked his wife and kids, and then he turned his attention to the two tables causing a ruckus in the back. What he said next helped explain why they were there, and it offered a reminder of how far he'd come on his journey as well.

"Those are my former Columbia football teammates, my long-term best friends and soul mates," he told the crowd. "And if we run out of wine at this dinner, it's their fault."

10

So What Have We Learned?
Lessons from the Last Guy Cut

*The most beautiful people we have known are those who have known
defeat, known suffering, known struggle, known loss, and have found
their way out of the depths. These persons have an appreciation, a
sensitivity, and an understanding of life that fills them with
compassion, gentleness, and a deep loving concern.
Beautiful people do not just happen.*
—ELISABETH KÜBLER-ROSS

SO THIS IS the part where I tell you how everything is
different now, how my adventures learning about losing
shaped my family and me in profound, life-altering ways.
How Charlie and Will are now model sportsmen, just the
appropriate level of competitive, always accepting their setbacks with a commendable dose of humility and perspective.
In the movie version, there would be a climactic rematch
between Charlie and his tennis nemesis, Jake, in which
Charlie loses in a third-set tiebreaker, jumps over the net,
and raises Jake's arm into the air like a triumphant prize-
fighter.

Of course reality is seldom so dramatic. My boys have
heard me talk about losing and failure a lot, to the point I
fear I talk about it in the way people talk about CrossFit, or

good places to eat near the Tampa airport—you don't even have to ask me. I talk about the merits of losing at dinner and on car rides and after baseball games when Charlie goes 0 for 4 with a throwing error. He spent a summer playing up a level, as a ten-year-old alongside boys eleven and twelve. Heady stuff, except he didn't hit a ball out of the infield the entire two months. I tried to sell him on the idea of it building character, in the same way Columbia football players started to see something beyond their 0–10 record each fall. Those messages need time to take hold.

One Sunday afternoon in November, Will's hockey team of seven-year-olds hosted a team from Brooklyn that comprised the children of Russian immigrants who darted around the ice like hummingbirds. They were aggressive, too, to the point that every time Will touched the puck, a couple would converge on him and nudge him into the boards. Will grew frustrated, his face reddening. At one point, the referee, not knowing the relationship, skated over to the bench. "That kid is about to lose it," he told me as their coach. He was right. After losing the puck one too many times in the third period, Will skated by the bench right to the door that headed to the locker room and marched off the ice. He was done. Other parents smiled politely in that "Thank God it's not our kid" sort of way. I doubt any of those parents were talking to their kids about losing half as much as I had been.

So the process is ongoing, yet I've grown convinced the lessons I explored these past few months serve a vital purpose. To understand the benefits of losing is to recognize how it touches every aspect of our lives—not just the games where we keep score, but the type of challenges we confront routinely in our careers and our relationships. Having submitted to this gospel, I plan to continue preaching it to my kids in an exhaustive, potentially irritating way. The more eye-rolling the better. They might not admit it, but I know they're listening.

Is there a risk in harping too much on negative outcomes? I get that sometimes. In discussing my topic with a friend, she mentioned how the last thing young people want to hear is that they're bound to fall flat on their face. It's too negative a message, she said. People at that age would prefer to be inspired. But what is inspiring if not a reminder of our pliability? What better way to fortify ourselves against the disappointments of adulthood than to be reminded that disappointments don't need to last?

As inspirations go, my boys and I love the movie *Miracle*, which is the true story of the 1980 US Olympic hockey team that upset the powerful Soviets en route to the gold medal at Lake Placid. For hockey players, it is almost required watching, but I'd argue it's a gripping tale for anyone, the story of a collection of obscure college hockey players who banded together to beat maybe the greatest team to ever play. The Americans, too, had to learn from losing. One of the movie's pivotal moments is an exhibition game days before the start of the Olympics in which the Soviets rolled over the US 10–3. It was evidence of the great team's superiority but also instructive for the rematch days later.

It really is a remarkable movie. I suggest you watch it now. Go ahead. I'll wait.

Anyway, one of the movie's bit characters is an affable forward with a thick Boston accent named Ralph Cox. Ralph had shaggy hair and a handlebar mustache, and in college hockey, he was a prolific goal scorer. The problem is Cox also suffered an ankle injury in the run-up to the games, and it continued to nag at him as the Americans were paring down their roster for Lake Placid. In another emotional scene in the movie, the US coach, Herb Brooks, calls Cox into his office to relay the news that he had to make one more cut, and Cox was it. Brooks was a tough guy, usually about as emotional as a hockey puck, but it was apparent that having to cut Cox gutted him, which makes sense: twenty years earlier, Brooks was the last player cut from the 1960 Olympic team that went on to win a gold medal.

In the aftermath of the 1980 Olympics, the players who went on to win the gold medal were given ample opportunity to bask in their improbable win against the Soviets. Along with the movie, there have been books and documentaries, as well as a steady schedule of public appearances. The player who scored the game-winning goal, Mike Eruzione, never played another competitive hockey game and has spent years trading off his celebrity at countless charity golf outings and corporate events.

Ralph Cox, meanwhile, became a curious footnote. When the US hockey team beat the Soviets, he was in

Tulsa, Oklahoma, having already started his professional career with a minor league affiliate of the NHL's Winnipeg Jets. Torn over whether to watch the game or pretend to ignore it, he put himself in front of the TV in an effort to get on with his life. He never suggests it was easy.

"Those were dark days," Cox tells me. "The hoopla, the parades. It was the toughest time to keep my chin up. I was embarrassed. I felt like I let a lot of people down."

With time, though, Cox forced himself to construct a new narrative. He had spent six months with the National Team prior to the Olympics, and he chose to be grateful for the role he had played in the team's subsequent success. He thought of his father, who had signed up for the service at age seventeen, and who had to endure the horrors of World War II in the Pacific islands. Compared to that, could Ralph really let himself be defined by being cut from a hockey team?

In the months and years following the 1980 Olympics, people often felt compelled to offer Cox their sympathies, but he rarely let them finish the sentence. "I would tell them, 'This is not the last chapter of my life,'" he says.

Approaching sixty, with a happy family and a successful career in commercial real estate, Cox now talks about his dismissal from the Olympic team as a kind of hidden blessing. Even more striking is that he never used his Olympic letdown as some vengeful fuel. When discussing Brooks, who died in a 2003 car crash, Cox still recalls how visibly painful cutting him was for the coach. When it comes to the teammates who tasted glory without him, Cox has only been a cheerleader.

"Right from the get-go I felt an obligation to all the guys to live life with my chin up and always be proud of their accomplishments, which I was," he tells me. "It took about ten years to truly realize I would do it all over again if given the chance. Don't get me wrong, I would have loved to be an Olympian. But I've had such a remarkable life, I couldn't imagine it being any better."

The definition of inspiring can vary. Certainly one type of inspiration can be found in a movie like *Miracle* that describes the most improbable of victories. But another is the lesser-told story of a man able to extract happiness and meaning from a crushing defeat. And to be clear, Cox *was* crushed by the abrupt end of his Olympic dream. If you recall, at the beginning of this book I mentioned a subject likening his defeat to George Bailey's in *It's a Wonderful Life*: "grief and desperation oozing from his face, wondering if there is really a good next step." That was Ralph.

"Having to find my way out of the darkness was at times a very painful experience, but ninety-five percent of it was incredibly powerful," Cox says. "Failure, if done properly, is the magical opportunity to create success and happiness."

THINK ABOUT HOW easy it would be for Ralph Cox to resent the guys who scaled the podium in his absence at Lake Placid, or to say how Brooks never gave him a fair chance. When I've been cut from teams before, that's been my default mode. "Politics," I would say, as if the varsity baseball coach who cut me my junior year got his orders from J. Edgar Hoover. Cox, meanwhile, is a testament to constructive "framing"—not to mention the potency of a "growth mindset." I've thrown a lot of terms at you, and don't worry, there won't be a quiz later. But even so, perhaps a refresher is in order.

What have we learned? We've learned through these stories that it's still OK to want to win. This book is not advocating we throw out the scoreboard and hand everyone a participatory ribbon instead. A common trait among the people we met in this book is the ambition to succeed. Greg Norman wanted a Masters green jacket. Michael Dukakis wanted to be president. Susan Lucci put on a dress and headed to the Emmys not because she wanted to flaunt her indifference, but because she hoped to hear her name called. The enemy of losing in a constructive manner is not winning. It is dejection; it is reaching that "Why bother?" point where we become too disheartened to even make the effort.

There's a quote from the author and motivational speaker Jack Canfield I've always liked. "Don't worry about failures," he says. "Worry about the chances you miss when you don't even try." Even better is one from that noted sage (and my personal hero) Wayne Gretzky: "You miss 100 percent of the shots you don't take." Both men essentially make the same point: The fear of failure is often more damning than failure itself.

Still, one problem with the way we pursue our ambitions is we tend to define winning too narrowly. It's why peak performers learn to channel their energy toward a process rather than a tangible goal. Think of Dan Jansen pushing himself in workouts and then writing dutifully in his training log. In his work with Dr. Jim Loehr, the mission for the skater became not to capture a gold medal but to feel satisfied that he remained committed to a process. With this as a focus, the end result became less daunting.

"As cliché as it sounds, there has to be a measure of success if you've done everything you can do," Jansen told the writer Jerry Barca in 2011. "What else can you do? You can train as hard as you can train and go out there and try your very hardest. There's no more that you can do."

Our ability to define success is a reminder that we are the final arbiter of what happens to us. Life doesn't come with a running scoreboard, and while we are certainly influenced by the standards of others, the ultimate gauge of our progress comes from within. Jansen and Loehr's contention is that even if the skater fell in his final Olympic race, he had avoided failure based on how wholly he committed himself to their plan. This is effective framing, and it permeates throughout the stories in this book. Columbia football players were able to frame their winless careers in a positive light because of the way it prepared them for postcollege life. The CEOs of failed startups could look back favorably at their abandoned efforts because these defeats provided a crash course in business that no MBA program could rival. All exemplify how we can construct a narrative around our experiences that can be more palatable and hopefully more useful. What was Ralph Cox doing when he decided not to be bitter about being cut from the Olympic team? He was writing a story that allowed him to feel better about one of the most painful episodes of his life.

"If you create a story that basically faces the truth but gives you hope for the future and inspires you to work harder, that's a story that can take you where you want to go," Loehr says. "That story can really be a pathway to something that would have never happened had you not had those failures."

Writing our own story does not invite the invention of new facts. None of this can happen without a generous helping of the truth. If I double-faulted two dozen times when losing a tennis match, am I doing myself any favors by declaring I served great? If our objective is to take something constructive away from a setback, then one needs to take an honest inventory. If you recall, the distinction between loss and failure is that one is a fact, the other an interpretation. When we lose without failure, it is because we are determining the loss fell outside our control. Sara Hess's soccer career ended because she blew out her knee and suffered all sorts of medical complications in the aftermath. That wasn't failure as much as it was rotten luck. These are the occasions when we deserve to be absolved of blame.

Often, though, the line is blurry. The turning point in the 1988 presidential race was when the George H. W. Bush campaign began targeting Michael Dukakis's perceived weaknesses—his soft record on crime, his thin national security record. Remember the commercial mocking Dukakis in a tank? At times it got personal, and it would be very easy for Dukakis to say he was merely a victim of dirty campaigning. Decades later, though, Dukakis doesn't see it that way. His failure was in not responding to the Bush attacks. The fault, he says, lies with him.

So THE BIG question is: How? How do you become the type of person who can turn losses into opportunities, who is clearheaded and strong enough to not let unwanted outcomes fester in counterproductive ways? The simplest answer is that we decide to be that type of person. Maybe it doesn't need to be much more complicated than that. There's a line that the former baseball commissioner Fay Vincent used when talking about how he responded to falling off a window ledge and breaking his back.

"When it happens, what choice do you have?" Vincent said. "You can either sit home and suck your thumb and feel sorry for yourself, or you can say there's something you can do."

That last part—"there's something you can do"—is easy to forget, particularly for those people who don't consider themselves resilient. That, too, is a mistake. When the psychiatrists Steven Southwick and Dennis Charney studied people's resilience, they figured that it was an inherited talent. Either you had it or you didn't.

"We assumed that resilience was rare and resilient people were somehow special, perhaps genetically gifted. It turns out, we were wrong," Southwick, a professor at Yale, writes in "The Science of Resilience," a follow-up article to their book on the topic. "Resilience is common and can be witnessed all around us. Even better, we learned that everyone can learn and train to be more resilient."

To recognize that resilience is a skill one can cultivate is evidence of the type of growth mindset that Dr. Carol Dweck stresses as so vital. The Stanford professor also believes our traits can be developed, and that losing and failure represent the best opportunities of all. Think back to her study in which researchers gave a group of fifth graders an easy test, praised half for their effort and the other half for their intelligence. In a subsequent more difficult test, the kids praised for their effort came to embrace the challenge. The ones praised for intelligence just wanted reassurance that they were smart and were disheartened when they began to feel otherwise. What happened to these kids? How could they diverge so sharply? It wasn't as if they fell under some spell. What happened is the kids praised for their effort were made aware of *their role* in the whole thing. They recognized effort as something they could control, which is an empowering feeling.

"They came to understand it's about more than the outcome," Dweck says.

A growth mindset is the key that unlocks a lot of doors. It shifts the emphasis away from results and toward that all-important process. It allows us to see the merits in every slip-up—getting cut from a team, botching a presentation, missing a train—because somewhere in there are the hints to how we can be better. Trust me, I'm not trying to pass it off as some magic elixir. If you're like me, you still come away from these episodes salty and pissed off, with some self-pity mixed in for good measure. But by the time I lay my head down at night, I find I'm able to recognize some good.

That's the other part. I went into this trying to teach my boys about growth and losing. I was merely the guy taking notes. When you turn forty, it's easy to entertain thoughts that this is who you are, that you've reached some kind of limit, with your only growth in the form of waistlines and lists of nagging responsibilities. I hadn't quite given into this type of thinking, but having met enough guys my age who do think this way, I see how quickly one can fall off the edge of that cliff.

What this journey reinforced to me is that there is no end to our growth. I probably won't make it to the NHL, but I'm presented daily with opportunities to be a better husband, a better dad, a better person. At *Golf Digest* we work in a media world of perpetual change, words on a page giving way to words on a screen, and now with slide-shows and animated GIFs, video and Snapchat. Ours is now a growth mindset industry, and not because it is pop-ulated by a group of inherently enlightened people. But most of those people recognize that to not grow and adapt is to render yourself irrelevant before lunch. We try a lot of things online and many of them fail, and we could conceivably fear looking stupid in the process. But we take notes, move on, try something new in the afternoon. It's the only way to stay sane through an era of unprecedented upheaval.

"Many industries are transforming constantly and things are becoming obsolete at a record pace," Dweck says. "If you are totally threatened by it and it's totally undermining your feelings of self-worth, you're going to find yourself struggling."

A decade after she first published her book, Dweck's teachings about growth mindsets have been widely influential. But they've also been misinterpreted. For starters, it's wrong to think we are all one thing or another, as if there's some box next to our name that declares us "fixed" or "growth." We all have fixed and growth mindset tendencies that compete within, which would explain why I can be frustrated by an outcome at first and then philosophical about it later that night. A colleague of Dweck's in Australia goes so far as to have his students *name* their fixed mindset personas, an acknowledgment that these tendencies have a way of butting into the conversation without invitation. To look at it in a very meta way, one of our chronic struggles is in how we deal with struggle.

"The first step is to acknowledge that we're all a mixture, that we have a fixed mindset in some situations, and really get in touch with it," Dweck tells me. "Start paying attention to what triggers that mindset. How do you feel when confronted with a challenge? Are you feeling defensive? Insecure? Threatened? When confronted with someone who is better than you at something, are you feeling diminished, or are you feeling inspired?"

Everything is a process, our mindsets included. In the same way that we can't expect to win every game, we also can't expect to see the lessons gift wrapped with every defeat. You'll still throw your racket and honk your horn, and at work, you might slam down the telephone receiver so hard that it will require an embarrassing conversation with IT (OK, so that was just one time). There is a moment in the movie *We Bought a Zoo* when the Matt Damon character receives some bad news and, in a fit of frustration, kicks over a barrel. Then he realizes that he needs the barrel and picks it up. That moment is what I'm talking about. At some point we all have to pick up the barrel.

On a rainy January day, Charlie, Will, and I were watching football. Charlie had a hockey game soon, but it was the playoffs, and the Vikings had to make a twenty-seven-yard field goal to win the game, so we stayed for the finish. When the kicker Blair Walsh hooked his attempt left of the goal posts, ending Minnesota's season, the scene was familiar, Walsh ripping off his chin strap, Viking coaches and players all staring in disbelief, the slow-motion replays reliving the final gaffe in grisly frame-by-frame detail. It was the type of excruciating Greg Norman moment that sports faithfully delivers several times a year.

Later there were reports of how Walsh handled the moment quite well—how he said the fault was only his; how he visited a first-grade class in Minnesota that had written him letters of support. But in the immediate aftermath of his kick, I could only speculate what was going through his mind. On our way to the ice rink, I asked Charlie how he thought Walsh should feel.

"Probably really bummed," Charlie said. "But maybe he can watch video or something to see what he can learn from it."

It was a great answer, even if there was a decent chance he said it knowing it's what I wanted to hear. We had been talking about this stuff for a while, and my perceptive son was at least smart enough to recognize my consistent theme about the great gift of losing. Give me a little more time and he may even start to believe it.

Acknowledgments

The most important teacher I ever had was a gifted novelist named John Yount, who as my college writing professor, first infused in me the notion that one day I could write a book people would want to read. We talked a lot about writing and books, Yount and I, and he once described his disciplined approach to his craft: waking before dawn, writing into the afternoon, then stepping away from his desk to head outside and chop wood. This was in many ways my ideal for writing a book. My actual experience, with a full-time job, a hectic family life, and an axe nowhere in sight, was vastly different.

This book is the sum of a great number of people's cooperation and patience, and while often a frenetic and taxing process, it is an experience I will always cherish.

Thanks to my agent, David McCormick, who helped an unproven author mold a rough concept and a few whimsical pages into something more substantive, and who shepherded me through the various anxiety-ridden stages of the publishing process. I'm grateful as well to my editor at TarcherPerigee, Stephanie Bowen, who enthusiastically took this book on and deftly helped refine the manuscript into the finished product you have before you.

My *Golf Digest* family was unfailingly supportive, but a few people stand out: Veteran authors David Owen, Matt Rudy, Dave Kindred, and Jaime Diaz endured countless questions about the mysterious world of agents and editors and provided essential feedback and encouragement. Bob Carney, in my mind the ultimate growth mindset, was perhaps the earliest supporter of this project. Tim Rosaforte remains a trusted mentor and friend. Mike O'Malley and Pete Finch provided guidance and smart edits.

I am fortunate to work closely with a passionate and nimble group at GolfDigest.com who understood I was balancing my day job with this behemoth project always in the back of my mind. Thanks to Alex Myers, Liz Bergren, Joel Beall, Keely Levins, Stephen Hennessey, Heather Brown, and John Strege for making me look good and at least feigning interest when I slipped into pretentious discussion of "my book." A special acknowledgment to Ryan, Lisa, and Caroline Herrington for reminding me the real meaning of strength through adversity. Perhaps most important, I am fortunate to have close to ideal bosses in Jerry Tarde, Molly Baldwin, and Chris Reynolds. Thanks for never blinking when I said I wanted to add this onto my plate, and for allowing me the freedom to do it.

Of course this book is nothing without the cooperation and candor of the people in it. There are too many to name, but they all tolerated an endless string of phone calls, coffee meetings, and emails, and did so fully embracing the message and mission of the book.

Thanks to the inventors of the iPhone for allowing me to occasionally write this book on a crowded subway car.

Finally, I am blessed to have grown up in a family with a mom, dad, brother, and sister whose bottomless love have provided me the confidence and security to withstand risk and occasional stumbles. My parents, Jerry and Sandy Weinman, were insightful readers of this text, and I knew if they didn't like something, they'd tell me. They, along with my amazing mother-in-law, Wendy Seaver, and late father-in-law, John Quirk, are my models for raising the two boys who are currently asleep in their beds as I write this. Charlie and Will Weinman were the inspiration for this book and its guiding light. They provided me endless material, ample comic relief, and daily reminders of how fortunate I am to be their dad.

One last piece of advice about losing is to get yourself a good shoulder to cry on. I've got the best. Lisa Quirk makes my life whole. Thanks for giving me a second look all those years ago and for being by my side every day since.

A Note on Sources

The bulk of reporting for this book was done through dozens of interviews with the subjects profiled and the people who could help illuminate their story. The second category was drawing on previously published work by journalists and experts, which I cite throughout the text. In a few instances, I relied on other works for background purposes. Even if I didn't quote the work directly, these books were invaluable in helping me understand a subject, an idea, or a time in history. Those works are listed below.

Coffey, Wayne. *The Boys of Winter: The Untold Story of a Coach, a Dream, and the 1980 U.S. Olympic Hockey Team*. New York: Crown Publishers, 2005.

Cramer, Richard Ben. *What It Takes: The Way to the White House*. New York: Random House, 1992.

Farrell, Andy. *Faldo/Norman: The 1996 Masters: A Duel That Defined an Era*. London, 2014.

Feinstein, John. *A Good Walk Spoiled: Days and Nights on the PGA Tour*. Boston: Little, Brown, 1995.

Frankl, Viktor E. *Man's Search for Meaning*. Boston: Beacon Press, 2006.

James, William. *The Principles of Psychology*. New York: Dover Publications, 1950.

Lahey, Jennifer. *The Gift of Failure: How the Best Parents Learn to Let Go so Their Children Can Succeed*. New York: HarperCollins, 2015.

Longman, Jere. *The Girls of Summer: The U.S. Women's Soccer Team and How It Changed the World*. New York: HarperCollins, 2000.

Lucci, Susan. *All My Life: A Memoir*. New York: It Books, 2011.

Roberts, Jimmy. *Breaking the Slump: How Great Players Survived Their Darkest Moments in Golf—and What You Can Learn from Them*. New York: HarperCollins, 2009.

St. John, Lauren. *Shark: The Biography of Greg Norman*. Nashville, TN: Rutledge Hill Press, 1998.

Vincent, Fay. *The Last Commissioner: A Baseball Valentine*. New York: Simon & Schuster, 2002.

About the Author

Sam Weinman is the digital editor of *Golf Digest*. Previously he wrote about professional golf and the National Hockey League for the *Journal News* in Westchester County, New York, where his work was honored multiple times by the Associated Press Sports Editors and Golf Writers Association of America. He lives with his wife, Lisa, and sons, Charlie and Will, in Rye, New York, where he coaches multiple youth sports teams.